Praise for

A Year of Mystical Thinking

*'If you want more magic in your life – and who doesn't,
quite honestly? – this book is a great place to start.'*
CLOVER STROUD, SUNDAY TIMES BESTSELLING AUTHOR OF THE
WILD OTHER AND MY WILD & SLEEPLESS NIGHTS

'This is so inspirational!'
LEAH WOOD, ARTIST, INFLUENCER AND ACTIVIST

*'This book is the mystical companion you never knew you
needed! There for every moon, reason and season – with
Emma's beautiful open heart and voice as the treasured
hand that leads the way with power, spirit and grace.'*
EMMA LUCY KNOWLES, AUTHOR OF THE POWER OF CRYSTAL HEALING,
YOU ARE A RAINBOW AND THE LIFE-CHANGING POWER OF INTUITION

*'A practical yet urgent call to cherishing life's potential
and pulling one's self out of the seemingly mundane
and into the magic that lives all around us.'*
ALEXANDRA ROXO, BESTSELLING AUTHOR, TRANSFORMATIONAL COACH AND TEACHER

*'This book captures the plate-spinning of modern life
and never-ending 'motherload' with humour and style,
offering up mystical practices that slot right in to the above
for anyone ready to turn up the magic! I loved it!'*
NATALIE LEE, CREATOR OF STYLE ME SUNDAY

'*An* Eat Pray Love *for the rest of us,* A Year of Mystical Thinking *is one woman's journey to finding the magic that lies outside of our comfort zone. This book is a call to those of us who are wanting to live a magical life and it's also an instruction manual on how to actually do it!*

Filled with entertaining, funny and relatable stories as well as deep spiritual guidance and wisdom, this book is the kindling that will relight your inner spark and help you to see the magic in the world and in your life again. A must read for anyone who's looking for their own magical adventure and a deeper connection to heart and soul.'

VICTORIA 'VIX' MAXWELL, AUTHOR OF *WITCH, PLEASE,* THE *ANGELS AMONG US ORACLE* AND THE *SANTOLSA SAGA*

'Modern life drives most of us to distraction at times, but this book might just be the antidote. An inspiring, funny and relatable mix of ancient wisdom, modern magic, and enough enticing astrology to pique anyone's interest! I'm recommending it to everyone!'

ALICE BELL, ASTROLOGER FOR *BRITISH VOGUE*

'Down-to-earth, frank, humorous spirituality. Packed with great ideas but without taking itself too seriously! Love it.'

CLEMMIE TELFORD, AUTHOR OF *BUT WHY?,* HOST OF THE *BUT WHY?* PODCAST AND CURATOR OF MOTHEROFALLLISTS.COM

A YEAR OF MYSTICAL THINKING

A YEAR OF MYSTICAL THINKING

Make life feel magical again

EMMA HOWARTH

HAY HOUSE

Carlsbad, California • New York City
London • Sydney • New Delhi

Published in the United Kingdom by:
Hay House UK Ltd, The Sixth Floor, Watson House,
54 Baker Street, London W1U 7BU
Tel: +44 (0)20 3927 7290; Fax: +44 (0)20 3927 7291
www.hayhouse.co.uk

Published in the United States of America by:
Hay House Inc., PO Box 5100, Carlsbad, CA 92018-5100
Tel: (1) 760 431 7695 or (800) 654 5126
Fax: (1) 760 431 6948 or (800) 650 5115; www.hayhouse.com

Published in Australia by:
Hay House Australia Pty Ltd, 18/36 Ralph St, Alexandria NSW 2015
Tel: (61) 2 9669 4299; Fax: (61) 2 9669 4144; www.hayhouse.com.au

Published in India by:
Hay House Publishers India, Muskaan Complex,
Plot No.3, B-2, Vasant Kunj, New Delhi 110 070
Tel: (91) 11 4176 1620; Fax: (91) 11 4176 1630; www.hayhouse.co.in

A catalogue record for this book is available from the British Library.

Tradepaper ISBN: 978-1-4019-6288-3
E-book ISBN: 978-1-78817-584-5
Audiobook ISBN: 978-1-78817-611-8

10 9 8 7 6 5 4 3

Interior illustrations: Mystical Thinking eye logo on jacket and
throughout interior by Agatha O'Neill.

Printed in the United States of America

Magic is real

CONTENTS

Prologue: In Pursuit of Magic   xi

Introduction: The Tarot Cards in the Basement   xiii

January: Vision Boards & Downward Dogs   1

February: Sound Baths & Spirit Guides   21

March: Everyday Magic   43

April: It's Just a (Moon) Phase   65

May: Don't Hate, Meditate   81

June: Play Your Cards Right   93

Six Months In   115

July: Garden Shed Healers & Crystal Myths   117

August: Written in the Stars   145

September: Empaths, Intuition & Indecision   161

October: Magical Places & Manifestation   185

November: DIY Magic & Spiritual Activism   199

December: Solstice Celebrations & Seasonal Living   215

New Year's Eve 2018   228

Epilogue: My Mystical Life   230

Spiritual Sourcebook   241

Acknowledgements   257

About the Author   259

Prologue

IN PURSUIT OF MAGIC

Ever had one of those years?

Haven't we all?

Ever wished you could run away? Step off the hamster wheel? Start over? Or escape to a far-flung corner of the planet in search of inner peace?

Sometimes it feels as if modern life has got us over a barrel.

Do this. Wear that. Be this but not that. Work harder. Run faster. Get thinner. Live better. Stand in line. Wait your turn. De-clutter. Fix your hair. Look younger. Be happier. Go to therapy. Speak the truth, but not *that* truth. Earn more. Buy more. Save up. Splash out. Don't stop. Try harder. Get up. Go out. Shouldn't you be recycling that?

Be cool. Be kind. Be quiet. Don't be boring. Don't let yourself down. Don't show yourself up. Have some wine to take the edge off. Do your bit. Make a difference. Quit while you're ahead. Save up for a rainy day. Stop slacking. Keep working. Finish what you started. And don't forget to smile.

Exhausted? Me too. Slip in a stressful life event and it's easy for the whole charade to come tumbling down. Burnout here we come.

But what if it didn't have to be that way? What if we could break the spell?

What if we could make life feel magical again?

And what if that magic felt modern and cool, fun and easy, exciting and accessible? What if you didn't need to go on a month-long silent retreat or shell out for a motivational self-help seminar? What if you asked the universe for your heart's desire and the universe obliged? What if you tried to understand yourself better and actually liked what you found? What if you let something go and something better appeared in its place? What if you trusted your intuition and found out it was right? What if you learnt how to cast a spell and understand the stars?

What if you found inner peace right where you are? No one-way ticket to paradise required…

Introduction

THE TAROT CARDS
IN THE BASEMENT

There's only one place for a dramatic New Year's Eve declaration as far as I'm concerned and that's my university WhatsApp group:

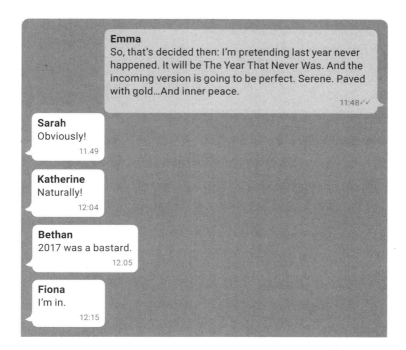

Sarah
What's the plan with the whole inner peace thing, Emma?
12:22

Emma
Well, I'm thinking I'll kick things off with a yoga retreat, then fly to wherever it was in Bali that Elizabeth Gilbert got her *Eat, Pray, Love* on. Then I'll meditate on a rock for a couple of months, neck some ayahuasca, and finish with a solo trek somewhere treacherous for the final epiphany.

I'm not walking as far as Cheryl Strayed did in her book *Wild*, though. I should probably also give up wheat or something, right?
12:40✓✓

Fiona
Sounds 'fun'.
12:42

Bethan
Don't skip the Italy part of *Eat, Pray, Love*! And DON'T DITCH WHEAT, FFS. I'm sure it was the pasta that actually soothed her soul.
12:44

Fiona
What the hell is ayahuasca?
12:50

Sarah
Maybe you can give all your money to one of those American motivational gurus while you're at it.
13:00

Emma
What money?
13:01✓✓

Katherine
What are you going to do with the kids while you're pissing about on a rock finding yourself?
13:08

Emma is typing...

Begin again

Someone once told me that if you lose your way in life, you should look back to what lit you up when you were younger. I wish I could remember exactly *who* because those words kicked off a year that changed my life.

A year that began with a quest to find inner peace but ended up changing everything. A year that turned frantic chaos into life in the slow lane. A year of magic and moonlight and pink-sky sunrises. A year fragranced with incense and burning herbs (that smelt suspiciously illegal).

A year that saw me get my chakras aligned in a garden shed and meet my spirit guide in a London loft. A year that filled my house with crystals and aura sprays and magic potions. And turned me into one of those people who are always banging on about the moon. A year that caused my husband to question my sanity on more than one occasion.

A Year of Mystical Thinking.

But let's rewind for a moment – to the end of 2017, The Year That Never Was. Because back then (and I know we've all been there) I'd never felt more broken. Exhausted. Burnt out. Just. Plain. Done.

I'd been struggling to adjust to life in a small town in Kent, in the southeast of England, having relocated from the southwestern city of Bristol for my husband's job as a doctor. Our new house was a building site and my two daughters were living on microwaved spaghetti hoops, served in a bedraggled corner of the attic.

I missed the buzz of inner-city living. I missed my friends. I was living on the wrong side of London for a Yorkshire girl, and my family in Leeds had never felt further away. I'd no idea how to find my people in the corner of 'banker belt' suburbia I'd crash-landed into. I felt like I was sleepwalking. I joined ladies who lunched (on air and rosé) for HIIT classes with prosecco chasers. I had a pumpkin facial peel. I started thinking I needed Botox. And fast.

Everything about me felt off-kilter, wrong, not quite good enough. I didn't fit in and I knew it. I'd overcommitted at work, and fitting my hectic magazine job in around school hours, holidays and hangovers was giving me palpitations. It felt like too much and not enough at the same time. I slipped back into habits I'd long since left behind – I was mainlining biscuits one day then juice fasting the next – and I was living for wine o'clock.

I felt constantly tired and lost and anxious. But I didn't tell a soul. Because when I wasn't feeling those feelings, I was feeling guilty. I knew that in so many ways, I had it all. But having it all in the modern world means spinning plates from dawn till dusk, right? I was already spinning a few too many when my husband's father died and everything came crashing down. And when the aftermath of that crash became a suffocating feeling that settled deep in my chest, I was terrified. Because I'd felt that feeling before…

At 12, when my best friend turned out to be pure frenemy. At 13, when my desire to fit in with the cool girls threatened to swallow me whole. At 23, when my parents got divorced. At 27, when health anxiety convinced me I would succumb to everything from breast cancer to HIV. At 32, when new motherhood hit me like a ton of bricks. At 35, when I solo-parented a baby and a toddler while my husband worked in a hospital 100 miles away. At 37, when I packed up the life I loved, in a city I loved, and started all over again in commuter-belt Kent.

I'm not trying to claim that this story is special. It happens to be mine but it could just as easily be yours. Because one thing is certain: I'm not the first person to experience anxiety or depression. Or struggle to deal with the pressures of modern life. Or contort myself while trying to fit in. Or feel guilty for not being happy despite being *#blessed*. I'm not the first person to see someone I love bereaved. Or be bereaved. Nor am I the first person to doubt myself or berate myself or stare into the middle distance wondering what the point of it all is. And I know I won't be the last.

Stories are how we make sense of the world.

I've spent my career as a journalist telling stories for magazines and newspapers and I believe we all have one to tell.

Our own unique reality. Our own version of the truth. You might see yourself in my story and I might see myself in yours. And sometimes, the flickers of recognition we find in those stories feel something like relief – connections and parallels that shine a light on who we are and show us that we're not alone. But we'll come back to that because at this point in my story, I was ready for a plot twist.

As I began to claw my way out of the doom that had settled over 2017, that advice about looking back to what had lit me up when I was younger began to repeat in my head like a mantra. Who was I before I became what I am? Before I was a writer, before I was a mother, before I was a wife or a homeowner or a hotel reviewer or an inept PTA member or a half-hearted Instagrammer? What were my childhood passions? Where did I once find peace? What *did* light me up when I was young?

That question was running through my mind when I stumbled upon a pack of cards hidden beneath some old photos in a box in the basement. My old tarot deck. Cards gifted to me when I was 14 years old and the world seemed full of potential. Tarot cards that I'd read regularly for well over a decade – foretelling friends' love affairs and exam successes as I sat cross-legged on teenage bedroom floors and threadbare flat-share sofas.

I must have put the deck in the box when I moved from one London rental to the next, some time before I turned 30, and then moved that box around with me, uninvestigated, for years. And yet I was rediscovering the cards now! It was as if they were a portal to a lighter past, at the end of the heaviest year.

I wondered if I could still read them. I gave the deck a shuffle and pulled myself a card. The Wheel of Fortune: the card of change and destiny. Every story needs a light-bulb moment, right? This was mine. And there and then, with a dismantled cot-bed and an unopened wedding fondue set as my witnesses, I made a decision.

Before I became all of the things I am today, I was a kid who knew what she believed in. I was an eight-year-old eco warrior (thanks to the hole in the ozone layer). I was an 11-year-old vegetarian (thanks to the supermarket meat counter). And by the time I was 14, I'd decided I was a witch. Astrology and tarot cards and love spells and midnight walks under vast starry skies – *that's* what lit me up when I was younger. Magic. Mysticism. The power of the universe. The great unknown. If I wanted to find inner peace in the here and now, this was surely where I'd find it.

Once the realization had hit me it all seemed so obvious. Of course – this was the beginning of a spiritual journey! A modern-day quest for inner peace. If I wanted to make the noise stop, I had to make a change. I needed to start living again.

I was brought up an atheist so I'd never believed in God, but I needed something to believe in now. I needed to step off the hamster wheel of busy, busy, busy and tap into something ancient and wise and meaningful. I wanted life to feel magical again. But how?

A year of *Eat Pray Love*-ing on far-flung shores sounded pretty ideal to me. I could see myself – unshackled, barefoot and free, doing sun salutations at dawn on a beautiful beach. I quite fancied a *Wild*-style solo trek through the wilderness, too. Nature and beauty and thinking time galore.

I'd read and loved and felt inspired by those two memoirs and their truth-seeking female authors. I also liked the idea of throwing a load of money at the problem and getting someone with serious spiritual credentials to just sort out my goddamned life.

But back to that reality check WhatsApp chat with my friends... Because *none* of those things were going to happen. I had a job and a husband and two daughters and a diary that was packed to bursting with parents' evenings and dental appointments and soft-play centre birthday parties. I wouldn't be jetting off to find myself anytime soon, and I didn't have the funds for gurus or spiritual life coaches or motivational weekend retreats. I'd have to find a way to change my life without bells or whistles or grand escapes from reality. So I came up with a plan.

 I set myself the challenge of fitting at least one mystical adventure into my regular, everyday life every month for a year.

Some of these adventures would be voyages into the unknown, trying things I'd never done before, while others would be about rediscovering mystical practices I'd let slide or had left forgotten in moving boxes for decades. I'd mix it up. I'd remain quizzical. I'd see the funny side. And I'd definitely keep it real. No purple robes or midnight chanting or blind belief or dramatic declarations.

I'd squeeze in yoga sessions after my children's bedtime. I'd meditate between meetings. I'd swap nights out for reiki sessions and celebrate birthdays at sound baths. I'd start where I was and I'd use what I had. And if something was free, easy, or possible to do without leaving the house, all the better.

So that's how my mystical year began.

In January, I made a vision board and did wobbly tree poses at the back of a new yoga class. In February, I discovered crystal sound baths and hung out with my spirit guide. By March, I'd assembled a mystical tool kit of lotions and potions and herbs. In April, I learnt to live by the cycles of the moon.

By May, I'd decided I was ready to become a master meditator. I spent June shuffling my tarot cards and July contemplating crystals. For most of August, I gazed at the stars. In September, I found a way to never agonize over a decision again, and in October I realized that nearly all of my January vision board wishes had started to come true.

I spent November learning reiki and December feeling calmer, clearer and happier than I ever had before at that crazy time of year. Best of all, I'd actually found the inner peace I'd been looking for. My mystical year had worked!

The next chapter

Which means we've reached the part where you and your story come in. Because whoever you are, wherever you are and whatever life's thrown at you, your story matters too. And you're the one who gets to write the next chapter. I'm not going to pretend to be a spiritual teacher or some kind of guru (I'm neither), but I wrote this book with you in mind. And I'd like to think you're reading it for a reason.

This is a story with one central idea: that the path to inner peace doesn't have to be spectacular or dramatic or backdropped by Balinese rice fields. That you can discover the magic of the mystical world without going on an expensive yoga retreat, spending all your cash on psychic readings or burning your belongings and living in a cave.

You don't have to disappear somewhere sunny or master meditation or become a perfect human being. You don't have to be young or cool or live in a city full of hipster crystal shops. You don't even need to have much time on your hands. And it really doesn't matter if you've never stepped on a yoga mat in your life. Or you never want to.

This book is about discovering *your* path to inner peace. Because, as I'd learnt for myself by the end of my mystical year, all the answers you seek are already within you. You just need to slow down for long enough to find them. And trust that you've got your own back.

This process of slowing down and tuning in can take many forms. Some things will help. Some things won't. Some practices will make you cringe in horror. Others will feel like one long exhale.

The mystical world is overflowing with tools that can help inject a little magic into the everyday.

By sharing with you the practices and processes that worked for me – as well as those that didn't – it's my hope that you'll find your own kind of magic (no 12-month sabbatical required): a way to buffer life's stresses and rise above its strains. Perhaps you'll also find something you can believe in. Because this is just the beginning.

Whether you devour this book from cover to cover or dip in and out of it on a whim, I'm pretty sure you already know the ending. Because inner peace is an inside job. The mystical world is having its moment, and there's never been a better time to make life feel magical again.

Magic of the month

At the start of each chapter of this book you'll find a list of magical correspondences for the month ahead: a seasonal celebration day; a moon of the month (I've used Native American Algonquian full moon names as it's those you'll hear referenced most often in the media and in everyday life); the astrological sign of the month (I've used the zodiac sign that the sun is in at the start of each month); a crystal of the month; the element of the month (earth, air, wind or fire) and a tarot card of the month.

You may like to use these correspondences as the inspiration for altar set-ups (more on these as you read on), or as starting points for celebrations, or just as gentle reminders of the ebb and flow of the changing seasons.

January

VISION BOARDS & DOWNWARD DOGS

Celebration: New Year's Day

Moon: Wolf moon

Sign: Capricorn

Crystal: Garnet

Element: Earth

Tarot: The Devil

Picture this

'Everything that exists was once only imagined.'
DR WAYNE W. DYER

I was determined to do New Year differently this time round. No schedule of tasks to tick off in pursuit of a lofty five-year plan. No punishing fitness regime. No pretending that compressed cauliflower has any place masquerading as a pizza base.

I was ready to kick the lingering sadness of 2017 to the kerb. Ready to move forwards. Ready to swap overwhelm and anxiety and the unsettling feeling that I just didn't fit in, for an aura of calm and inner peace. I was ready to embrace a brave new world – one that called for a more mystical way of setting my intentions for the year to come than a classic list of resolutions.

I started 2 January 2018 by pouring half a bottle of prosecco down the sink (because even when I'm doing things differently, I like a Dry January cliché) and gathering together the tools for my very first mystical adventure. Which is how I found myself hunched over the kitchen table later that night, tearing my stash of magazines into aspirational pieces as the first full moon of the year cut through an overcast sky.

I was creating a vision board – a cut-and-paste glimpse of glories to come. A paper collage of words, images and inspiration that would manifest into magical reality. A visual blueprint for my Best Life. Something like that, anyway.

I'd seen plenty of vision boards before (they've become an Instagram mainstay) but I'd never made one myself. And I wasn't sure where to start. Nor could I quite shake the feeling that this was all a bit Noel Edmonds circa 2006. (Cosmic ordering – the belief that we can all achieve our goals by adopting a positive mental attitude and asking the cosmos to deliver! Didn't we all laugh at him for that?)

How the hell was it meant to work, anyway? Should I just stick a picture of a Tulum beach house and four million quid on a sheet of cardboard and wait for the universe to deliver? As with most things in the mystical realm, it turns out there's no one right answer.

Some anthropologists have theorized that prehistoric cave paintings were in fact the very first vision boards – depictions of shamanic visions designed to bestow magic on the hunt. Swap bison and warthogs for pay rises and swanky handbags and not much has changed in 40,000 years. The principles behind the vision board remain the same: if you can dream it, you can achieve it – as long as the cosmos has got your back. Which is where the 'magic' comes in.

Ever heard of the Law of Attraction? Or manifestation? Or attempted to make it to the end of a god-awful film called *The Secret* on Netflix (or read the bestselling self-help tome by Rhonda Byrne that followed it)? Well, the principles behind these concepts are how vision boards are said to work.

 The Law of Attraction asserts that like attracts like, and that you will attract into your life whatever you place your focus on.

The basic premise being that your thoughts and feelings have the power to change your reality. So, if you *believe* that something wonderful is going to happen, it *will* eventually happen. And if you *believe* that your life is rubbish and it's going to stay that way, that's exactly what you'll get.

Now I'm not saying I buy into *all* of this. I can think of multiple scenarios and life situations that would be impossible to turn around with positive thinking alone. Plus, it's pretty reductive (if not plain offensive) to suggest that someone's misfortune is inevitable simply because they have negative thoughts.

But I'm also prone to overanalysis, overthinking and procrastination so I stopped all that before I talked myself out of the mission. In the spirit of my new approach to life, the universe and everything, actions would speak louder than words. I wouldn't allow myself to cast doubt on the task at hand before I'd even started. I'd simply get to work. After all, there was a Mexican beach house to manifest.

Taking the time to make a vision board provides the space required to focus the mind, get clear about our goals and intentions and really tune in to how we want to feel and the way we want to live our life. And when that positive feeling vibrates out into the universe, well, that's where the magic happens – that's how you get one step closer to making your vision a reality. I'm pretty sure that having a visual reminder of what you're aiming for pinned on a wall must help things along a bit too.

I set to work at a frenetic pace – so much for slow and mindful. Once I'd settled on the idea that my creation would be the blueprint for my year, I wanted it done, and fast. My focus was razor sharp. When my eight-year-old daughter, Lola, decided she wanted in on the cut-and-paste action, I was too engrossed in my vision to even think about interfering. I just let her go to town on the glue and glitter and unicorn pictures (*seriously, kid, you're never going to own a unicorn – get over it!*), while my mind wandered happily in my own future wonderland.

I laid out a large piece of yellow card on the kitchen table and printed out photos of beaches and sunsets that made my heart beat faster. I sought out images that symbolized activism and freedom and a slower pace of life. I cut out pictures: my two daughters silhouetted against a pink sky on a jetty in Greece; a woman smiling beatifically alongside a neon peace sign; a hiker resting on a bench overlooking the dreamiest of mountain views; a retro camper van parked on a deserted beach.

There were a few more specific images too: a quote saying 'You deserve good things'; the front cover of a magazine I'd always wanted to write for; the word 'fun'. And some slightly more superficial pictures of home improvements and expensive slip dresses (hey, why not!?), plus a wad of cash for good measure.

I felt that adding some words to my creation would give it a bit more gravitas; however, after some less than enlightening searches on Google for ideas, I realized I'd have to make up my own rules. Before gluing the images onto my vision board, I wrote down everything I wanted to invite into my life on one half of the card and everything I was ready to let go of on the other.

A favourite playlist on the speaker, a cup of soul-soothing herbal tea (every bit as good as gin, I told myself) and a dedicated hour of grown-up cutting and sticking… Don't knock it till you've tried it.

I was surprised to feel the power of my vision board almost immediately. Even as I sat cutting out pictures and imagining my perfect, stress-free future, I found myself remembering the times in my life when I'd made things happen with nothing more than wishful thinking.

There was the school trip to France when I willed a room mix-up so I could infiltrate the cool girl gang. It worked. I ended that week with a stash of Vogue cigarettes in the pocket of my denim jacket and an invitation to hang out by the toilets in the car park the following weekend (believe me when I say this was the pinnacle of early teen interaction in the small Yorkshire town I grew up in during the 90s).

Then there was the sort of 'fake it till you make it' positive visualization I did before every job interview, exam or presentation for years. I think I spent more time visualizing myself getting my job at *Time Out* magazine in 2006 than I did thinking about how I'd answer the second interview questions. I already knew that I'd get the 'yes' call the minute I exited the building. I was right, too: the universe delivered my dream job.

Maybe I was getting swept away by it all (my enthusiasm for January fresh starts will never die). But then…

I felt more positive and powerful just making my vision board, so who knew what wonders lay ahead?

I decided to use that night's full moon to add some extra magic to my creation – I stuck the board in the brightest window I could find and left it overnight. And by the time I un-tacked it the following day and propped it up on my desk, I was pretty convinced the universe was already doing my bidding.

It didn't take long for the first signs that this was true to trickle through, either. Just a few days later, my mother-in-law Erini announced that she wanted to relive some of her favourite travel memories with her late husband and was booking a family trip to Sri Lanka for later in the year (*sunsets, beaches… tick*).

Then an editor contacted me about working on a feature for a magazine for which I'd never written (*not the one on my board, but still an amazing opportunity*); and finally, the builder we'd contacted about putting up some shelves in our living room unexpectedly found a free slot in his schedule (*so the universe even had my frivolous home improvements goals covered – result*).

I couldn't quite believe it. The vision board was actually working. And it wasn't even the end of January. Call it beginner's luck or blatant overenthusiasm but I felt more at one with the universe already. And I was pretty sure I'd be rolling around in a massive wad of fifties before the year was out.

Which brings me to the next part of this story. Because this isn't really about *my* vision board – it's about yours. And it's about *you*. You taking your own moment in time to think about what you really want out of life. You gathering your thoughts, allowing yourself to dream big and visualizing your most magical future.

What if you really could have everything you've ever wanted? What would your life look like if there was nothing holding you back? What would you do if you could do anything? What would you do if you had nothing to fear?

Do it yourself – create a vision board

Your vision board can be anything you want it to be. There are no limits and no rules. You can plaster it with images of couture and sports cars, or pictures of family and friends, or far-flung destinations and inspirational quotes. It doesn't even have to feature images – it can be as simple as one key word or a phrase in 72-point type stuck on your fridge so you see it every day.

Your vision board can be digital, if you prefer that to a physical version. Or it can be a beautifully crafted visual masterpiece in tones that match your sofa. It really doesn't matter. What matters is that you take the time to make it and that every time you look at it, you feel positive, fired up and inspired. If it does that, it should be doing its job in the cosmos, too.

Here's how I made my vision board; feel free to adapt this method to suit you.

What you'll need

- A large sheet of card or paper (A3 size or bigger)

- Pens, glue, scissors

- Magazines and newspapers; print-outs of inspiring images; photos that you love

- A candle, an aura spray or incense to set the space and focus your mind *(optional)*

- Blu Tack, or another reusable adhesive *(optional)* – I used this to stick my board to the window overnight!

♦ A full moon *(optional)*. I chose to use the power of the full moon because there happened to be one on 2 January 2018 when I made my vision board. Full moon is said to be a good time to let go of anything that's holding you back in life, but it has the power to sprinkle some magic on dreams and wishes too. You could also make a board on a new moon, as this part of the lunar cycle is ideal for intention setting. And you can, of course, make one any time of the month you like! See the April chapter for more information on harnessing the power of the moon.

How to do it

1. Draw a large infinity symbol – essentially a sideways number 8 – on your sheet of card or paper.

2. Light your candle or incense and sit quietly for a few minutes before you begin. Take some deep breaths and on each exhale, focus on letting go of negative thoughts, old ideas, or anything that might be holding you back.

3. In the right-hand side of the infinity symbol, write all the things you wish to call in/the intentions you want to set for the year/months ahead. (You're going to cover up all the words, so let them flow freely – without worrying about priorities or typos or the horrific embarrassment of someone seeing that you're trying to get the universe to deliver a second chance with your wayward ex).

4. Repeat the previous step on the left-hand side of the infinity symbol, this time writing everything you'd like to let go of in the coming year/months.

5. Take a photo of your vision board before you move on to the next stage – in case you forget what you wrote.

6. Cover the whole sheet of card or paper with beautiful, inspiring images that appeal to you, whether or not they're related to your goals and intentions.

7. If you wish, Blu Tack your vision board to a window (images facing outwards) so the light of the full moon can shine on it, charging it up with extra cosmic magic. You can do the same on a new moon, but there won't be any shining light as this is a dark phase of the moon.

8. Put your board somewhere you can see and refer to it in the months to come.

9. Await the magic!

Back on the mat

> 'Yoga is a light which once lit will never dim.'
> B.K.S IYENGAR

Once my vision board was safely pinned in daily view and my fridge was stacked with alcohol-free beer, there was one more thing I knew I had to add to my mystical January. Downward dogs are to spiritual journeys as gin is to tonic (not that I had booze deprivation on the brain or anything) – I needed to get my yoga on.

If I kicked off this part of the chapter by telling you that I've practised yoga since the late 1990s, you'd get the wrong impression entirely.

There are no perfect handstands or crow poses on my Instagram feed (or if there are, it's not me in the picture).

I've studied under no gurus nor partaken in any lengthy retreats. In fact, I only started doing yoga in the first place because I was trying to impress a rollerblading hippie History student I met during Freshers' Week at Liverpool University. He'd spent a gap year in India (the birthplace of yoga), bringing back with him with a penchant for tie-dye, headstands and spiritual superiority. And for some reason I found that wildly appealing.

The six-week course in hatha yoga I embarked on that October lasted way longer than our relationship. But the relationship I began with yoga looks like it's going to last a lifetime. Which once again makes me sound way more polished than I am. Bear with me here. Yoga is not about polish.

I've always leant towards the sick-note side of sporting activity: I've no hand–eye coordination, team sports make me think everyone hates me and I'm still reeling from my discovery that the point of tennis isn't to get a rally going. When I finally gave running a go aged 34 – after two babies and a lifetime of skinny-girl laziness – the resulting all-over muscle pain was so alarming I considered a trip to A&E.

I've upped my fitness game since, but no one could describe me as overly invested. In fact, the only form of physical movement I've ever felt any real affinity with is yoga. Discovering it on that course in my university's sports hall was a light-bulb moment for me.

The teacher, Patricia, was calm and wise. I'd never met anyone like her before. She was in her sixties (I discovered while researching this chapter that she's actually still teaching yoga in her eighties), had been teaching for over a decade and practising yoga since she was a child. She was measured, radiant, otherworldly. She knew stuff. She was a great advert for making yoga a part of your life and sticking with it. Better still, I'd finally found a way of moving my body that wasn't about winning, beating the other team or nailing a personal best.

Despite what some studios or gym-based classes would have you believe, yoga was never meant to be focused solely on physical movement (the *asanas* or postures). Its original purpose was to cultivate awareness, harmony and higher consciousness; however, co-opted by the Western world, it often feels as if it's more about the abs. Observe the content of some yoga classes and you'd have no idea that there are eight limbs to this ancient practice (none of which require the creation of an Instagram account) or that it originated in India rather than LA or Primrose Hill.

I'm no expert on yoga – nor am I immune to the glossy allure of marketing – but when I'm keeping it real in my threadbare leggings it helps me to remember that that's kind of the point – yoga was never meant to be about the shiny stuff.

> *For me, the best thing about yoga is the way it enables me to quieten the noise of my overthinking mind.*

Have you ever tried stressing about something you once said in a meeting while holding a half-moon pose? It's impossible!

I may not have been the most committed yogini in the years that followed that first class in Liverpool, but when I really needed it, yoga was always there. After-work ashtanga got me through a copywriting job that bored me to tears in my twenties, and pregnancy yoga with Bristol's earthiest earth mothers offered me an instant community when my husband's medical training necessitated a move from London to the southwestern city just after I turned 30.

It would have made sense if I'd used yoga to smooth the transition when we were uprooted once more – this time from buzzy, urban Bristol to suburban Kent – but I didn't. Instead I attempted to fit in by following the Joneses into hardcore HIIT classes and fancy lunches and endless conversations about shopping and home improvements and Range Rovers. None of which made me feel any better about my new life situation. It also meant that when the shit hit the fan in 2017, I had no regular yoga class to soothe my stressed-out soul.

So, making sure I got back into yoga was a no-brainer for my mystical year. I just had to find the right class. Nothing too sedate: been there, stared out the window. Nothing too intermediate: my 20-something self did that class for years and it ended in flexibility angst and competitive starvation. Nothing too peppered with enlightened statements about 'honouring oneself' or 'stilling the waters of the pelvic bowl'. No dusty community centres (not the right vibe). And no morning classes: they always end in me making a To Do list in *shavasana* (the prostrate relaxation pose at the end of a session) instead of clearing my cluttered mind.

I needed the Goldilocks of yoga classes – one that was 'just right'. And once I bothered to look properly, that's exactly what I found. I signed up to a candlelit Monday evening session at a beautiful studio overlooking a wood. The teacher, Helen, was funny and down-to-earth, the kind of person you could imagine going for a drink with (if you weren't doing Dry January). The class was a short walk from my house and there were good vibes galore – and no annoying 20-something versions of myself to contend with, either.

Much as I had with the vision board, I felt the benefits of yoga immediately. Muscle memory kicked in. I was rusty and inflexible but that first class felt like one big exhale. I was back in the room (and also hiding at the back of it), on the mat, breathing, moving and knowing instinctively that this was going to do the trick, as it had so many times before.

I felt my jaw unclench and my whole face relax. I may have even stilled those pelvic waters. There were no perfect crow poses or anything remotely worthy of an Instagram post, but that was never the point. A couple of classes in and I felt less stressed, less anxious and way less chaotic. The short meditations at the beginning and end of the class tapped into a sense of stillness I rarely experienced in my day-to-day life. I began to notice the return of a grounded feeling that I'd long forgotten existed.

By the end of January, four classes in, I felt as if I had life nailed. I was eating all the green stuff, drinking nothing but water and sleeping like a baby. My body was a temple. I was cool, calm and collected. On one school run I felt such indescribable joy at the sight of a sky filled with perfect fluffy clouds that I no longer recognized myself. I was ridiculous. But those clouds *were* perfect! And I was happy for the first time in months. Was this inner peace? Had I pulled it off in the first few weeks?

Do it yourself – discover yoga

I've already imagined that this is the part of the book most likely to be skipped over, simply because so many people have already made up their minds about yoga. Possibly, you included.

It could be that yoga is already a massive part of your life, and you've studied with the masters. You might even be getting ready to roll out your mat right now. This whole section might be preaching to the converted. In which case, great.

Or perhaps you tried yoga once and didn't like it? Or you thought it was too slow and boring? Or you dismissed it because it doesn't burn enough calories to 'count'? Maybe the studio you picked felt cliquey?

Maybe you've never tried yoga. Perhaps you think it's not meant for people like you, or that you're not thin enough or young enough or bendy enough? If that's the case, I hear you. From lotus pose Christy Turlington on the front cover of *Time* in 2001 to Gwyneth Paltrow extolling its virtues to anyone who'll listen, yoga in the West can present as a homogenous activity. One-size-fits-all, if you will, just as long as your size is rich, white and thin. It's no surprise that many people feel put off or excluded before they even begin.

Fortunately, times are changing. There will always be gyms selling yoga as a fitness-focused class, but it's becoming easier to find studios that demonstrate awareness and respect for yoga's history and its origins as a spiritual practice.

It's also easier than ever to find role models that break the bendy white-girl mould. Take the *#everybodyyoga* movement promoted by US-based Jessamyn Stanley, for starters. She began posting yoga pictures on Instagram in 2012 and published her first book, *Every Body Yoga*, in 2017. Her 'The Underbelly' online courses aim to be as inclusive as they are inspiring.

There are plenty of other teachers doing their bit for inclusivity, too. Canada-based Dianne Bondy, author of *Yoga for Everyone*, is on a mission to ensure that everyone feels they can practise yoga, regardless of their shape, size, age, ethnicity or ability. In the UK, Nahid de Belgeonne, creator of The Human Method, has made waves with her mindful, restorative, somatic take on the practice. And modern yogi Ravi Dixit draws upon years of study and a childhood spent practising yoga to offer authentic and accessible hatha classes in London and Goa.

Even if you've been put off yoga in the past, you'll hopefully find that approaches have changed in your hometown, too. Today, there's a trend towards community classes and beginners' sessions, as well as low-cost options for those on tighter budgets, and way less focus on the hardcore 'advanced' classes of past decades.

Styles of yoga

If you take time and care when choosing your studio or teacher you should be able to find a class that feels respectful, inclusive and a good fit for you. Below is a brief guide to some of the most popular styles of yoga

Ashtanga

An energetic style in which a specific series of poses is followed in order, punctuated by *vinyasas* (transitional movements such as the half sun salutation).

Hatha

A (usually) gently paced class with an emphasis on breathing and holding *asanas* (poses).

Hot yoga

A challenging class in which poses are practised in a heated room.

Iyengar

An approach that places emphasis on careful and correct alignment using props such as blocks and belts.

Kundalini

A combination of intense movement, chanting, breathing and meditation designed to awaken energy in the spine.

Mysore

A self-practice type of ashtanga in which a teacher is available but not leading the class – great once you've learned the basics.

Nidra

A therapeutic practice involving extremely gentle movement, breathwork and meditation.

Vinyasa flow

A teacher-led class influenced by ashtanga yoga that flows freely from pose to pose.

Yin

Relaxing, restorative yoga that's mostly focused on passive or seated poses.

Reasons to give yoga a(nother) chance

So, as yoga in the West becomes more respectful and accessible, perhaps it's time you rediscovered its benefits or gave it a try? Your mind, body and soul will certainly thank you. If you need more convincing, read on.

Easy access

Yoga is everywhere, which means you won't find it difficult to find a class near you. You might have to shop around a bit until you find the right one, at the right time of day, that fits in with your life, but you *will* find one. And if a regular in-person class doesn't work for you there are some brilliant teachers offering online sessions you can follow for free at home – try Yoga with Adriene on YouTube – as well as books, podcasts and magazines to tap into for inspiration.

No gear, all the ideas

You don't need any special equipment to get started. A mat is useful for at-home practice, but it's not totally essential at first. If you choose a class in a gym or a studio there will most likely be a mat you can borrow. You can wear anything loose and comfortable in which you can move freely. You don't need trainers. Or a water bottle (unless you pick a hot yoga class). Or weights. Or expensive bum-sculpting leggings. You don't even need a sports bra.

Beginners are winners

In yoga circles, talk of the importance of retaining 'a beginner's mind' is almost as popular as the waters in the pelvic bowl thing. Yoga isn't about being the best or nailing the poses or doing anything faster or better than anyone else. Being a beginner is actually a benefit as it takes your ego (the cause of many an awkward headstand fail) out of the equation completely.

Time out

There have been times in my life when the idea of fitting in an hour-long yoga class seemed impossible, but I've come to realize that this is actually the point. Committing to a yoga class forces you to take some time out from the rest of your life. And a decent amount of time at that.

If you really don't have the capacity to reframe it in that way right now (parents of babies and toddlers, I've been there), there are shorter online sessions or simple at-home flows you can learn.

Body positivity

Modern life is hectic. We spend so much time in our heads – planning, analysing and overthinking – that we forget to check in with our bodies. Taking the time to practise yoga turns that around. You begin to notice how your body feels instead of how it looks.

Take a few moments *right now* to roll your neck or shoulders around – had you even *noticed* they were so tight? This sense of conscious physical awareness is a big part of what makes yoga different to other types of movement. You begin to feel at home in your own body. Which, let's face it, is the only one you've got. And with that comes acceptance, body positivity and greater self-esteem.

Health is wealth

The great thing about upping the body positive factor and building self-esteem is that you're way more likely to take good care of a body you've decided to love than one you're hell-bent on hating. It's well known that yoga builds strength and flexibility over time, but it can also change your approach to what you put into your body. I'm not going to claim that this is a hard and fast rule (I've walked out of a yoga class and into a bar on more than one occasion), but becoming more mindful about what you eat and drink often becomes second nature once yoga is part of your life.

Free your mind

The mental health benefits of yoga have always been my biggest reason to keep practising. It's impossible to overthink in the middle of a sun salutation. And a long *shavasana* at the end of a strenuous class is a great introduction to meditation. Then there's the breathing: I've learnt breathwork techniques through yoga that can get me through dental appointments, job interviews and the toughest toddler bedtime.

Instagram likes

And finally, if you're so inclined, no one is going to stop you from spending a fortune on shiny leggings and showing off your crow pose on Instagram. Sunrise backdrop compulsory.

See the January entry in the Spiritual Sourcebook at the back of the book for more resources and recommendations.

February

SOUND BATHS & SPIRIT GUIDES

Celebration: Imbolc (Brigid's Day)

Moon: Snow moon

Sign: Aquarius

Crystal: Amethyst

Element: Air

Tarot: The Star

Surround sound & 90s boy bands

'Are you sure this 'project' isn't just you paying
people to let you have a lie down?'
MY HUSBAND

Once I'd dipped a toe into the mystical world, it was as if I'd sent
out a bat signal for the rest of it to find me. The Mystical Thinking
Instagram account I'd started in January gathered a few followers
and the algorithm soon kicked in, linking me up with yogis, healers
and crystal dealers from Sevenoaks to Salem.

I'd spent years looking for my people and now here they all were,
posting inspirational quotes about the moon. At least that's what
it felt like. Inspiration was everywhere all of a sudden and I wanted
in on All Of It. The idea of swearing off resolutions and To Do lists
and The Cult of Busy was fast flying out of the window.

I'd acquired a Mystical To Do list and it was growing by the day.
The pile of books on my bedside table was out of control and the
spiritual FOMO was real. I'd planned to fit my mystical missions
calmly around my normal everyday life. But normal everyday life
felt dull in comparison to the new world I'd discovered. I wanted
to bare my soul at story circles and perform new moon rituals, not
unload the dishwasher and attend editorial meetings.

It didn't help that February is the craziest, busiest month of the
year for me, with my two daughters' birthdays, my birthday,
several close friends' birthdays (I like my people Piscean, okay?),
school half-term, and a magazine workload impacted by all of the
above (especially the half-term bit).

And, well, it's a bloody short month anyway, isn't it? I started to wonder if I even had the *time* to pursue inner peace. And what was the point of this mystical quest if it left me more frantic than I'd been when I started it?

My mind might have hit overload again, but I was determined not to give up on the mission. Throwing myself into as many offbeat therapies and interesting spiritual practices as possible was always part of the plan, and real life wasn't about to go on pause. I just needed to get a grip and prioritize.

There were mystical adventures I knew I wanted to go on, practices I wanted to tap back into or rediscover and workshops and events that seemed to appear on my radar like magic, at the exact moment I needed them most. Which is how during one mindless lunchtime scroll break, I stumbled across a dreamy-looking Insta square promoting a crystal sound bath session at a swanky London hotel.

I'd heard of gong baths but not crystal sound baths; and if I'm honest, the former had never really appealed. I'd seen adverts for sessions when I lived in Bristol and the mental image they conjured (flowing robes and eau de patchouli oil, anyone?) instantly put me off. I was also aware that sound can soothe the soul – crashing waves, birdsong, the first three bars of 'Dancing Queen' after precisely the right number of vodka tonics. But meditative, healing, relaxing? That didn't sound like something a gong would do for me. And delivered en masse in a dusty community centre? That was a straight up no.

Judgemental? Sceptical? Closed-minded? Yep, I was all three. But that was then. And this was now. And a sound bath featuring crystal singing bowls seemed like a different proposition entirely.

Perhaps it was because the Instagram post came courtesy of hippie dream girl Jasmine Hemsley, who was launching a crystal sound therapy venture called Sound Sebastien. Maybe it was the pleasing pastel aesthetics of the pearlescent pink, lilac and turquoise crystal bowls. Or did I just like the idea of my spiritual pursuits being served with a side of fancy hotel bar? Either way, I was sold.

The crystal sound bath session promised to be an immersive experience that would induce an effortless meditative state. Like many people, I find it hard to relax, so meditation can be more than a little frustrating. But I needed to chill out more than ever. My workload was off the scale and the mental load of parenting never seemed to let up. Within minutes of seeing that post, I'd booked myself and my friend Lucy into a Monday-night session as a joint February birthday celebration (I didn't ask her first).

I got stuck into a bit of online research (once a journalist always a journalist) and soon discovered that crystal singing bowls – or at least the pure quartz and gemstone bowls created by the brand Crystal Tones – are insanely expensive. This isn't something you can just DIY with a few mates in your living room.

 I also learnt that sound bath meditation is meant to be an ideal relaxation method for people who find it difficult to switch off.

The tones produced when the singing bowls are played (by running a mallet around the rim or tapping the side of the bowl, gong-style) are both heard and *felt* by the body, and these vibrations are said to have healing, soothing properties.

I also found some stuff about quantum physics that made my brain hurt as I skim read it, so I pushed it to one side. If bathing in sound could switch off my internal monologue for a while, I was all in – with or without the science bit.

'So, what is a sound bath, anyway?' Lucy asked as we swung a right off London's Oxford Street on our way to our night in the aural realm.

'Ah, well, it's all about quantum physics and the vibrations of the universe,' I replied.

She raised an eyebrow.

'Okay,' I laughed. 'I think it's basically easy-access meditation. A way of quickly altering your state of consciousness. Sound that you don't just hear but actually feel.'

'Like dancing next to a nightclub speaker?' Lucy asked.

'I reckon,' I said. 'We zone out. We tune in. And if all else fails, it'll be one hell of a posh lie down.'

On arriving at the hotel we nodded to the doorman and headed straight to the bar. I wasn't totally convinced that a pre-session prosecco was the right call (doesn't alcohol numb the senses?) but I wasn't going to say no. Plus, I was nervous. We watched as a trail of hipster millennials and 40-somethings in expensive activewear headed downstairs to the basement.

'These must be our people,' I declared.

'Isn't that Howard from Take That?' asked Lucy as she drained a champagne flute.

We wandered towards the hotel's basement (which had been a club called The Basement before local residents got it closed down) and once there, ditched our bags and shoes in semi-darkness. I felt my shoulders lower. It was already relaxing and we hadn't even started.

Dim lighting, calming aromas, soothing voices and rows of comfortable mats set out with neck pillows, white fluffy blankets and lavender-scented eye masks, like a massive grown-up sleepover. This was my kind of club night. We picked a spot a good distance from Howard (the quest for inner peace doesn't allow for 90s boy band distractions) and tucked ourselves in. You don't have to ask a mother to lie down twice.

Flat on our mats, blankets pulled up round our necks, we listened as Jasmine and Sound Sebastien's co-founder, Toni Dicks, explained what was going to happen (basically, we'd relax and they'd play the crystal bowls). We were given the opportunity to raise a hand if we didn't want to be repositioned, anointed with essential oils or have them use reiki on us during the session.

After a hectic Monday (think Sarah Jessica Parker in *I Don't Know How She Does It*, minus the high-flying career and power suits), they could have lobotomized me halfway through for all I cared, as long as I got to stay horizontal. What followed, though, was far more magical than a high-end power nap.

As the room settled into silence, I shut my eyes (lavender mask applied) and listened as we were talked through a simple breathwork relaxation. Easier said than done for the overthinkers among us: as the breath of the people around me became slow and calm, I ran through a quick To Do list, contemplated how I'd describe the room's aroma in a review, and wondered if I'd forgotten to press send on my last work email of the day. Right on cue, someone appeared to reposition my legs and dot calming oils in the middle of my forehead.

I concentrated on turning my focus inwards – as they say in yoga – and soon after, the sounds began. There were deep, vibrational tones that I felt in my chest (unsettling and not entirely pleasant at times) and higher-pitched sounds that felt lighter and more uplifting. As each tone vibrated through my body and faded away, another built in its place, creating a continuous reverberating, humming beat.

I felt myself chill out properly for the first time in months. For someone who struggles to switch off in *shavasana* and writes mental shopping lists when I'm meant to be meditating, this felt like a·miracle.

The sounds were all-encompassing and all I had to do was listen to them. And *feel* them, too. *That* was the element that really set this practice apart from all the other times I'd tried and failed to chill out on a yoga mat in a dimly lit room. There was something to *focus* on, but nothing that required conscious attention. Like magic, my brain had found its off switch.

Somewhere between this tranquil zone and the gentle rousing at the end of the session, I lost track of time, space and maddening thoughts completely. Instead, my mind settled somewhere peaceful, still and almost otherworldly. I wasn't asleep but I wasn't awake either. Wherever I'd been, I wanted to go there again – immediately. And every day from here on in, if possible.

Even just lying down for an hour was a revelation. I mean, when was the last time *you* relaxed for an hour other than in an attempt to sleep? During a massage or a facial, perhaps, but even a beauty treatment comes with the sense of ticking something off a To Do list. This was lying down and relaxing for relaxing's sake. It was a game-changer. Why don't we all do this, all the time? Or at least sometimes? Since when did resting become such a massive indulgence?

As tinkling chimes and a slow count signalled the end of the session, we sipped cups of herbal tea in silence.

'Out-of-body experience,' Lucy mouthed.

We blinked our way back into the real world, scanning for the reactions of our co-sound bathees. Universally blissed out, I'd say, especially Howard.

That blissful feeling lasted, too. The rest of the evening took on a surreal, zenned-out vibe. A series of perfectly timed black cabs, green lights and a train that left the station the second we stepped aboard were enough to convince me that the universe approved of our evening. Watching my party-girl friend opt for a peppermint tea over a gin in a tin for the journey home convinced me that sound baths had superpowers.

I felt cool, calm and collected well into the next day, too, despite a return to the mayhem that is attempting to combine work and half-term childcare. I'd discovered the swiftest and most intense path to a meditative state ever. Sounds baths were easy, relaxing and fun. I even found myself wondering if they could be the future of going out. This felt like the mystical buzz I'd been waiting for. I was hooked.

Do it yourself – soothe your soul with sound

The concept of sound as therapy turned out to be one of the biggest take-homes of my mystical year. I slipped in several more sound bath sessions as 2018 progressed, each as magical and relaxing as the one just described. But booking yourself an in-person crystal bowl session isn't the only way to access these therapeutic benefits. Here are a few different ways to tap into the magic of sound.

Crystal sound

You don't need any previous experience of meditation or special equipment to enjoy a crystal sound bath. Track down a practitioner in your local area and book a private one-on-one or group session. Turn up, lie back and let the vibrations take over. Many practitioners also run free and paid-for sessions on social media.

Binaural beats

Binaural beats therapy makes use of the fact that when you present the left and right ear with two tones of slightly different frequency, the brain perceives a third, different sound: a 'binaural beat'. Depending on their frequency, binaural beats are said to help reduce anxiety and induce sleep.

All you need to check them out for yourself is a set of headphones and access to YouTube, where there are many samples available. The Synctuition meditation app also has some brilliantly relaxing examples to try.

Get outside

Nature is the easiest-access sound bath of all. Even if you don't live in the countryside for blissful quiet or by the sea for crashing waves, get up early enough to hear birdsong (in your garden or through a window) and you've got yourself a free sound therapy session.

Playlist upgrade

Switch things up from the same old same old on Spotify or Apple Music. Try a relaxing spa playlist, listening to Kirtan (devotional chanting) or shamanic drumming. Any sound that takes your mind somewhere else entirely.

Sing-along

Try chanting, find a drumming circle, sing in the shower, join a choir. Being brave enough to share your voice or make music (especially in public) can be as joyful as it is therapeutic.

Play it again

Even if you can't stretch to investing in a set of beautiful crystal singing bowls there are plenty of accessible sound therapy instruments you can try at home. Tibetan singing bowls, healing tuning forks, HAPI drums, Koshi chimes, bells, rain makers – see what takes your fancy and give it a go.

Gong song

Don't dismiss a gong bath without trying one, like I did. This type of immersive sound therapy has been practised for thousands of years. As with a crystal sound bath you don't need any prior experience to join a session, just an open mind and a desire to lie back and feel the vibrations. Think easy-access meditation with transformative results.

For more recommendations and resources, see the February entry in the Spiritual Sourcebook at the back of this book.

☆

The elephant in the room

> 'What if your spirit animal turns
> out to be an amoeba?'
>
> MY FRIEND BETHAN

By the end of February I felt as though I'd lived a year in one month. I might have set the universe to work on my vision board – now stuck to my bedroom mirror so I could dream about sun-drenched beaches while applying industrial-strength concealer to the bags under my eyes – but inner peace still felt like something I wouldn't find anytime soon.

The sound bath buzz had gently faded and all the yoga in the world didn't seem to stop me from overthinking every little thing. I hadn't found myself enthralled by fluffy white clouds for weeks. My magazine job was busier than ever, and I was constantly running to keep up with friends, family and a never-ending cycle of laundry and homework and rejected fish fingers.

The sadness of 2017 felt even heavier as 2018 began to hit its stride and life, naturally, began to move on. I felt panic rising within me again. And after a successfully Dry January, I found myself once more blocking it all out with a glass of something potent at the end of each day.

I was anxious. And stressed. And so bloody tired. I couldn't see a way out. Friends who had been supportive began to fade back into their own busy lives – lives that seemed to be punctuated by endless dinners and lunches, captured by Boomerangs of clinking glasses that made me feel more alone than ever when I scrolled past them on Instagram.

I tried to organize something for my birthday, only to find that everyone I asked already had plans: with each other and without me. It was fair enough – I'd left it until the last minute, as usual – but that realization didn't help shake the nagging, empty feeling that I'd never fit in (and that everyone else knew that too). What I needed was some backup. Of the mystical kind. So that's what I decided to find.

Have you ever felt that you might have a guide in some otherworldly realm? An angel or an ancestor or a benevolent magical being: someone or something guiding you towards good decisions and keeping you out of harm's way? I have…

At 14, when I found myself horizontal and horrified at a house party with a much older boy and couldn't find the words to say *no*. But then a sudden interruption arrived like magic, allowing me to make my escape. At 16, when my friends and I ran in the dark towards the edge of a cliff in Devon, high on freedom and spontaneously procured LSD (thanks to more older boys). Until a voice from nowhere stopped me in my tracks, just before we crossed from life to death.

At 22, on the road to Alice Springs in Australia, when I looked up to find our driver friend asleep at the wheel and heading for an oncoming road train. Until my screams saw him swerve with seconds to spare. At 23, while swimming in a riptide on a deserted beach in Thailand. I still remember the heart-stopping panic and how the strength that powered me back to shore that day felt so much mightier than my own.

And then there's the early 00s. All-nighters in disused railway arches, dodgy minicabs, spiked drinks, stumbling home, shoes in hand – I sometimes wonder how my friends and I made it out of that hedonistic era in one piece. Unless, of course, we all had a spirit guide. It certainly felt that way to me.

On all of these occasions I felt as if something bigger than me had my back. Something that didn't want to see me plummet to an untimely death or pass out on a dingy street corner in an up-and-coming area of East London.

Perhaps we all have memories of moments in life that feel as if they could have gone either way. Sliding doors. The times we swerved death or escaped disaster or opened the right door instead of a very wrong one. Perhaps you see those moments as luck or coincidence or just something that happened randomly. I can see the logical side, of course I can. But I guess I've always been looking for magic.

The idea of spirit guides – protective universal forces – is common to many mystical and spiritual teachings, while spirit animals are of particular significance in some Native American traditions.

It's said that spirit guides are magical pathfinders, messengers, interceptors, helpers, show-ers of the way. Beings or entities devoted to our guidance and protection.

A divisive concept? Certainly! Easily rubbished by the sceptical? Erm, yes! Intriguing all the same? I think so. I mean, who doesn't like the idea of a spiritual sidekick who is 100 per cent Team You?

This was exactly the thought that passed through my mind when I spotted an online ad for a 'Meet Your Spirit Animal' workshop at a London yoga studio. In my witchy teenage years, I'd imagined that the rabbits in the field next to our house were a crew of familiars, animal guardians of some kind, but I'd never really contemplated the idea that there was one specific animal guide waiting to show me the way.

Was a shamanic meditation journey to discover my spirit animal a legit mystical adventure – or was this project making me go bonkers? I pushed the whole thing to the back of my mind and returned to speed-writing features about family gap years and alternative education choices for my magazine job. But something must have stuck because a few days later I found myself mentioning the session to my friend Laura, who surprised me by not laughing in my face and insisting we book ourselves in immediately.

And that's how I found myself drinking orange-scented cacao (a sort of healthy hot chocolate thought to have medicinal, heart-activating qualities) in a candlelit loft, ready to go on a two-hour guided journey with Tamara Driessen, a crystal healer, tarot reader and shamanic practitioner who also goes by the name Wolf Sister.

Finding the loft's location had proved to be quite the experience. We'd headed out on a freezing Sunday evening and there was a quiet, eerie feeling in the air. A car crashed right in front of us as we exited the Tube station, and we spent ages trying to find the venue, wandering the streets in the dark. I sent a pin drop to a friend showing our last known location, just in case we got sucked into another dimension, and as I did so, I realized I was only half joking.

I'm not sure what I thought a Wolf Sister would look like, but my overactive imagination was relieved when Tamara turned out to be the opposite of every stereotype it had conjured: barefoot and beaming, with long dark hair, an Essex accent, a fringed cardigan, and not a New Age cliché in sight.

As our group gathered blankets and notebooks and settled onto our yoga mats, Tamara explained what the next couple of hours would hold, her excitement so genuine that getting swept along with it was a breeze. As she talked about her experience as a shaman's apprentice in Bali – where she'd discovered her own animal guides during meditation – I became less sceptical and more intrigued.

Could that sense I'd had that something was looking out for me all those times actually be correct? I'd never thought of those guides in animal form before, but if Tamara believed it, why couldn't I? Or was this all just smoke, mirrors and suggestion? Imaginations in overdrive! Still, even if spirit guides are figments of our imagination, perhaps the part of the mind they come from has some sort of wisdom to share. Ten minutes in and I was already overthinking it.

Tamara then started talking about her Indonesian heritage, shamanism and the importance of knowing the difference between cultural appreciation and cultural appropriation. And of course, that set my mind into overdrive. I knew about cultural appropriation – Kim Kardashian in cornrows, Katy Perry dressed as a geisha, the unacknowledged or inappropriate adoption of a culture's ideas, or traditions co-opted by another, usually more dominant, culture – but I was ashamed to realize that it hadn't even crossed my mind when I'd clicked the 'book' button for this workshop.

I silenced my whirring thoughts for long enough to hear Tamara explain more about her training and practices and how the evening was going to work. The fact that this was the first time a wellness/alternative practitioner had mentioned cultural appropriation at a workshop I'd attended felt reassuring. This was something she clearly cared a great deal about and wanted to get right, and her wholehearted enthusiasm for the subject was impossible to ignore.

But my intrusive thought-reel was on a roll. How had I not considered cultural appropriation when I'd signed up for this? If spirit animals are a Native American tradition, was it better if I thought of them as guardians or familiars? Was I missing a trick here? And why the hell had my mind waited until I was already committed to pose a series of difficult questions on a quick-fire loop?

I tuned back in to the room in time to hear Tamara say that all we needed to do was lean in to our intuition, step aside from our egos and be open to what lay ahead. My ego was clearly an overthinking bastard. I was grateful for the wake-up call but I forced myself to put it to one side for the time being. I was already in the room and on the yoga mat and the session was about to start.

Tamara's voice began to draw me back in. She stood up to lead us in a ritual to call in the four directions (north, south, east and west). She then cast a sacred circle around us and asked us to lie down on our mats to begin the journey. And, well, you already know how I feel about lying down!

 According to Wolf Sister, we all have an animal spirit guide ready and waiting with messages and answers from another realm.

She explained that this might be an animal with which we've always felt an affinity, or one that's been following us around on street art or Instagram or gifts and cards given to us by friends and family. I wondered if mine had been following me around. I mean, I'd always had a thing for rabbits, but as far as I could remember, no one had ever given me a rabbit-related gift.

Is *your* special animal obvious to you? Perhaps you have a visiting backyard hedgehog or the world's biggest collection of ornamental pigs? Or perhaps you're contemplating skipping to another chapter? Honestly, I get it, but bear with me.

Tamara's voice was calm and lyrical and I soon got in the meditative zone. And as she talked us through our guided journey, I was surprised by how easily the visions came and how beyond my control they seemed. They really did feel as if they were emerging fully formed, without any input on my part.

I found myself walking on springy moss in the Yorkshire countryside, the air full of colourful butterflies. I followed a sparkling stream, passed through a cavernous tunnel lit by glow-worms and descended deep into the Earth in a red velvet-clad lift. These were all gently guided scenarios – Tamara would mention a descent or a body of running water but the detail came from within – that somehow spookily appeared one step ahead of her instructions.

Before I started I was pretty convinced that my animal would be a rabbit, so when I saw a few hopping about before I stepped into my velvet lift, I wondered if I was peaking too soon. But somehow, it made sense that I was leaving them (and possibly some of my preconceptions) behind.

As the journey continued, the landscape I found myself in became tropical, humid, hot and hazy. It was beautiful and I really didn't want to leave it behind, even if doing so meant moving on to the part where my animal would appear. But I tuned in and listened to Tamara's gentle guidance, slowly walking towards that big reveal.

As I did so I caught a glimpse of a young elephant between the trees my mind had conjured, but I didn't think anything of it. More than that, I actively rejected the idea that it could be my animal and assumed it was just part of the tropical scenery. I was still expecting that rabbit familiar.

Soon we were told that the time had come to meet our animal and I couldn't wait to discover what mine was. And, of course, in strode the elephant. No rabbits for me, after all. Tamara suggested we reach out and touch our animal, then ask it its name and if it had any messages for us. I felt kind of ridiculous hugging a spirit elephant in my mind's eye and letting it tell me its name was Rose (*I mean!*), but that's exactly what happened. And somehow, in meditation land, it didn't seem that weird at all.

Rose the elephant turned out to be pretty chatty, with many words of wisdom to impart. But the main message was loud and clear: I needed to recognize my own strength, have more self-belief, and allow myself to grow. Pretty clichéd, Rose, if you don't mind me saying, I thought. She also told me I should book a trip to Asia, although I'm willing to admit that part might have just been wishful thinking (*Hey, family, I'm off travelling because a mystical elephant told me to*).

I could happily have spent much longer getting the lowdown on life, the universe and everything from a giant talking land mammal, but all too soon, the journey was over. As Tamara talked us back into the room, I looked around the group, keen to know where my experience was going to fit in the scheme of things. Had everyone had such vivid visuals? Were they as freaked out as I was by just how real it had felt?

As we went round the room sharing the highlights of our journeys, our messages and our animals I was struck by how different everyone's session had been. There were mountain wolves and swooping owls, majestic butterflies, wisecracking anteaters and even a zebra in the mix. My friend Laura, who'd been lying on a mat just inches away from me and my tropical land, had found herself clad in fur up a snowy mountain with an arctic fox. Someone had found themselves flying through the air with their animal, never quite able to see its face. As Sunday evening chats with random strangers go, it was among the most fascinating – and surreal – I'd ever had.

The session ended with more cacao, oracle cards (a simpler version of tarot) for added insights, and time to sit and chat with Tamara and each other as we looked up the meanings of our animals in Ted Andrew's book *Animal Speak*.

Laura and I made our exit in search of dinner, and as we ate, we raised a toast to elephants, arctic foxes and how hanging out with your spirit guide is way more fun than Sunday night Netflix. I mean, you might think you've had some trippy experiences in life but until you've chewed the fat with Dumbo on a yoga mat, I really don't think you've seen it all.

The strangest part of the whole experience, though, came when I got back home and realized there were elephants *everywhere* in my house. The Ganesh painting my mother-in-law had brought back from India; a bizarre elephant ornament we'd been given as a wedding present that I simultaneously hated and refused to get rid of. Most of these elephants were in rooms I used often, too. My makeshift office has a picture of an elephant on the wall and a set of four painted wooden ones lined up on the windowsill.

I'd never been 'an elephant person', but soon I started to see them everywhere. I began to spot them on buildings I'd walked past blindly hundreds of times. I saw them on clothes, in paintings, in jewellery, on social media and occasionally in my dreams. I started to see them as signs: comforting gentle giant nods that I'm on the right path or making the right decision about something.

Sometimes, before I fall asleep, Rose the elephant pops into my mind unannounced. She doesn't talk, like she did that night on my yoga mat, but she stares at me, as if she's letting me know she's still here and she has my back – the elephant in the room.

Do it yourself – meet your spirit guide

Spirit guides don't have to be animals – they can be ancestors, angels, goddesses or other mythical or magical beings. You might feel that you already have one. But if you don't, or you're looking to expand your team, how can you find out who they are? And what does it all mean?

Guided meditation workshops

The easiest way to fast track a connection with your spirit guide is meditation. And a guided meditation (like the one described above) is the most straightforward method. To find a suitable local session, try a search on EventBrite or ask around on Facebook and Instagram. Once you've decided you're interested, these things have a habit of suddenly appearing on your radar.

Online meditations

Grab some headphones and sink into the sofa with an online guided meditation to help you connect with your spirit guide. Gabrielle Bernstein has a dreamy 16-minute meditation that's easy to do and YouTube is full of longer guided sessions. Have a browse, pick a meditation that appeals and do a quick 'first few minutes' check for infuriating music or annoying voices (both are deal breakers for me). Then get stuck in. There's something quite satisfying about ending a meditation session with bonus backup from the spiritual world.

Watch & wait

You don't even have to meditate to work out who your guide is, if you don't want to. Invite them to find you and they might appear in a dream. Or you might, as Wolf Sister explained, begin to see connections between certain images or characters that repeatedly show up in your life. If your world is covered in unicorn motifs (and not just because you're the owner of an eight-year-old), maybe that's your guide.

See the February entry in the Spiritual Sourcebook at the back of the book for more resources.

Ways to connect with your spirit guide

Once you've got yourself a spirit guide, what do you do with them?

Look up associated meanings

If your guide is someone you know, the sort of guidance they offer you might feel pretty obvious. Late grandmothers will want you to be safe, happy and following your dreams just as much as they always did. But if your guide turns out to be a mythical creature or a warrior goddess, you might want to look them up.

There are books, of course, but the easy-access option is Google. Discovering the qualities traditionally associated with a specific angel, goddess or animal you've found hanging out in the furthest reaches of your mind is the first step towards working out what they're here to help you with.

Journal

Freewriting is another great way to tap into the outer reaches of your mind. It can take a while to get the knack of this practice but the basic premise is that once you're in a relaxed state in which you've tapped into your subconscious mind (after a meditation, for example) you spend some time writing down whatever flows out through your pen. No overthinking, no careful spelling, no concerns about punctuation or grammar. Just see what your subconscious comes up with.

Start with the beginning of a sentence, such as, 'My spirit guide would like to tell me...', and see what comes out.

Ask them for help

Ask them to help you achieve your goals. Request that they show you the way. Make a wish. Write them a note and burn it to ash. Invite them to infiltrate your dreams. Ask them to show you a sign that you're making the right decision or choosing the right path. Your guide works for you now.

March

EVERYDAY MAGIC

⭐ **Celebration:** Ostara (spring equinox)

🌙 **Moon:** Worm moon

♓ **Sign:** Pisces

🔮 **Crystal:** Aquamarine

🔻 **Element:** Water

🃏 **Tarot:** The Moon

Routine to ritual

'Make the ordinary come alive... the
extraordinary will take care of itself.'
WILLIAM MARTIN. *THE PARENT'S TAO TE CHING*

There's a journalling exercise I like where you write 'In my best life I wake up and...' at the top of a piece of paper and then allow yourself to freewrite a stream of consciousness about where you'd be and what you'd be doing if it all went right.

I'm really into Best Life Me.

Best Life Me gets up at dawn because she's the type of person who doesn't just read about the morning routines of life's go-getters and then go back to hitting the snooze button, she actually makes it happen. Best Life Me meditates every single day without fail. And never gets distracted. Best Life Me rolls out her yoga mat and drinks green juice and practises gratitude like she invented the concept.

She lives in a pristine, organized and aesthetically pleasing house by the sea with her equally pristine, organized and aesthetically pleasing family. She always cleanses, tones and moisturizes. She doesn't bite her nails. She writes Christmas cards. She cooks from scratch.

She would never put on activewear at 7 a.m. with absolutely no intention of being active at any point that day. Hell, no! Best Life Me changes out of her Lululemon yoga pants into something floaty and bohemian plucked from a curated wardrobe of vintage finds. Best Life Me can throw words like 'curated' around without making you want to throttle her for being so annoying. She's *that* good!

Best Life Me never feels stressed out or overwhelmed or as if she's letting everyone down. She hasn't even heard of imposter syndrome. She doesn't lie awake at night berating herself for saying something inconsequential but awkward in a conversation that happened six years ago. She doesn't get FOMO or worry that the party is going on somewhere else without her.

She creates effortless vegan dinner parties using elegant glassware and plates that match. She never accidentally drinks too much rosé or tries to hog a karaoke mic. She knows which day the recycling bin gets collected. And she puts it out on time. If she owned a paddleboard (which she would, she's like that) she'd stand upon it looking elegant and serene. First time.

You get the picture. I'm into this exercise. And I'm really into Best Life Me. Shame that Real Life Me gets in the way. Shame that real life was getting in the way.

That saying about March coming in like a lion was ringing bleakly true. The weather was grim – snow had turned to muddy slush on the school run and the shades-of-grey mornings were dragon-breath cold. The footwell of my battered old Citroen had become a permanent water feature. Every radiator in the house was hung with damp gloves and scarves and the wet-dog aroma of drying wool permeated the air. Spring is meant to be the season of hope and new life but it all seemed a bit lost in translation.

My work had taken itself to the next level of insanity. I'd come to a slow-motion car-crash style realization that the part-time freelance gig I thought I could slip calmly into my life was actually taking it over. I'd overcommitted big time. It was physically impossible for me to fulfil my designated desk hours, write as well as I wanted to *and* do all the school pick-ups and holiday childcare and play dates and homemade sushi crafting that modern motherhood requires.

Or rather it *could* be possible, but only if I did nothing else. Ever. Including sleep. I needed a body double. Or to fake my own death. Neither of which seemed more easily achievable than just blindly ploughing on. So that's what I opted for. And, of course, that meant a few things had to slide.

Before the first week of March was done, my list of mystical adventure plans had disappeared under a pile of interview notes. I barely had time to sleep, let alone commune with spirit guides. I was answering emails during school ballet shows, scrawling notes on receipts in the car and arranging interviews on speakerphone with a nit comb in hand (I mean, seriously, universe: come on!) I'd started 30 Days of Yoga with Adriene on YouTube but was permanently stuck on day three.

I really wasn't sure if this whole spiritual quest was working out after all. I was still getting to my Monday-night yoga class and making my way through a stack of books with enticingly magical titles, but I didn't feel beatific or at one with the universe – and the only glow I had was blue and coming off my iPhone. Work stress, deadlines and never-ending emails from my kids' school about World Book Day were ruling the roost. And Best Life Me was missing in action.

I started to wonder if there was a way I could edge my life (the one with no paddleboard and an overflowing recycling bin) closer to the one my subconscious conjured when I allowed it to pour itself onto the page.

It was a tough call. I couldn't just run away to live in a perfect house by the sea. And telling myself to 'just bloody well get up earlier and juice stuff' felt way too reductive. We've all seen that meme which declares, 'You have the same number of hours in a day as Beyoncé,' right? And we all know that if it were that simple we'd have released our seventh album by now.

Nothing is ever simple when you've made commitments, stacked up deadlines and/or produced some small humans to worry about.

How was Best Life Me funding her serene existence, anyway? She hadn't bothered to slip that information into her whimsical ramblings! Regardless, I decided there must be a way I could tap into her cool, calm and collected vibe – a way I could make life feel more magical, right here, right now, before I lost the plot completely.

I thought back to those successful people and their high-flying morning routines. Wasn't that, ultimately, about carving out time to do the things they deemed important? Even if I didn't have the time (or the inclination) for a 5 a.m. power walk, perhaps I could turn small pockets of my day into something that felt less stressful and more meaningful. Could I find a way to turn my routines into rituals and the mundane into magic? Despite not owning anything by Lululemon, I decided to try.

Everyday rituals, spiritual quick fixes, mindful moments slipped into life as it happened – *that* would be my goal for March. I wouldn't always have the time or space for a big mystical adventure and I had to find a way to be okay with that. Anyway, wasn't finding magic right where I was the goal for this year? Maybe March had the potential to be my best month yet.

I started by picking a sign.

I'd reached the part of Gabrielle Bernstein's *The Universe Has Your Back* where she talks about choosing your sign. This is a symbol that either comes to you spontaneously or that you consciously choose, that shows the universe you're ready to collaborate. It can be an animal, a colour, a song, a scent, a series of numbers, whatever you like. Once you've picked your sign you can ask the universe to show it to you when you're on the right path or making good decisions or getting closer to a chosen goal.

I instantly loved how simple and easy this was – I mean, anyone can pick themselves a sign and wait for a high-five from the universe! The first thing that popped into my head was a rainbow, so that's what I chose. And just like magic, suddenly rainbows were everywhere.

Now, I'm not sure how this whole thing would work if what popped into your head was some rare Amazonian tree frog – basically, don't do that! However, if this seems like something you can get on board with, I'm sure the end result will be the same.

I began to find solace in seeing rainbows appear at magically perfect moments. The one that arched across the sky outside my window just after I'd braved a no in a work email when I knew my editor was anticipating the usual yes. The many rainbows that appeared in my Instagram feed every time I logged on to check my Mystical Thinking account – like colourful fist bumps urging me to keep going.

The refracted beams of rainbow light on the floor of the shower when I finally managed to get up as early as Best Life Me would, so I could have some time to myself before my girls woke up. Basically, it worked. And it was so easy.

 ✧ *Choosing your sign from the universe requires little effort and delivers an impressive amount of pay-off. Best of all, it feels good.*

I felt like I'd hit the jackpot straight off with a spiritual quick fix that buoyed my spirits in just the right way. Cosmic pats on the back that upped the magic factor of the most ordinary moments.

Next up, I thought about ways to add extra magic to things I do every single day anyway. Like drink a hell of a lot of tea.

Blame it on my Yorkshire upbringing, plain old caffeine addiction, or the procrastination opportunities presented by boiling a kettle multiple times a day, but tea is a big deal in my world. My day begins with a strong cup of Yorkshire Gold (milk, no sugar), ends with a fragrant mug of Pukka Night Time, and is punctuated by countless trips to the kitchen for chai or peppermint or chamomile in between. If you could find inner peace on tea alone, I'd have called off the search years ago.

I didn't think it'd be difficult to turn my tea habit into something that felt a bit more special. Tea ceremonies and rituals are nothing new, after all, dating back to China's Tang Dynasty (618–907). Fast-forward to today and the cultural and historical significance of tea is all around us. It's in popping the kettle on when a friend stops by for a chat, in the camaraderie of the office tea round, and in the tower of scones served with pots of loose-leaf English Breakfast at your best friend's baby shower.

You definitely don't have to travel far to get to grips with the magic of tea, but you'll soon have a cup in your hand if you do. Think sweet, spicy chai at a train station in India, mint tea poured into glass cups in Morocco, or the precise beauty of a cup of Japanese matcha. Tea is way more than just a hot drink: it's comfort, it's ritual, it's culture, it's magic.

I began by taking just a bit more time over it. I picked my favourite mug from the dishwasher instead of grabbing whatever was at the front of the cupboard. I cut down on my while-the-kettle-boils multitasking routine. I tried sipping my first cup of the day in screen-free silence. I stocked up on new varieties of tea at my local health-food shop and ordered a loose-leaf blend from a herbalist I met on Instagram. I added expensive herbal pyramid bags I'd normally consider off limits to my supermarket order. I poured hot water onto fresh mint leaves picked from the garden. I found ways to make tea even more of a pleasure than it already was.

I also began to tune in to the way different blends and herbs made me feel. I noticed the calming effect of chamomile sipped on deadline day and the warmth of ginger and lemon on chilly afternoons when I couldn't feel my toes.

My tea stash began to feel like my very own herbal apothecary, filled with mood-boosting fixes and soothing cures.

So far so good... But I fancied a bit more flourish, so I began stirring my intentions for the day into that first morning cup. And those silent wishes – stirred clockwise three times – certainly felt like magic. They helped focus my mind on what really mattered and pushed me to press pause for a while. Quiet spells cast with a teaspoon wand.

Despite gallons of tea and rainbows everywhere I was still mindlessly scrolling through my phone whenever it appeared in my field of vision, which just so happened to spark my next idea. The second I saw a dreamy Instagram shot of a flower-strewn *#ritualbath* I knew I had the makings of my next quick fix.

Don't stop reading! I'm not about to suggest you resign yourself to fishing petals out of the plughole for the foreseeable future, but I do think that upgrading bathtime (or shower-time – both work) is an easy win.

My Piscean soul has always loved a bath – the more potions poured into it the better. I once stopped a New Year's Day hangover in its tracks with nothing more than hot water and half a bottle of Dr Hauschka's Lemon Essence. And I've credited a peppermint, fennel and fir blend called Fortifying Green Bath Potion by the pleasingly named Magic Organic Apothecary (an independent British brand) with curing everything from colds to bad moods to heartache.

Salts, bombs, scented oils... I'm here for the lot of them. I'm not sure I'm even capable of writing the words *long, hot soak* without wanting to go press the 'extra hour button' on the boiler. So, as far as bathtime was concerned, I was already a convert – I just needed a way to switch it up.

It didn't take me long to find my answer. I discounted most of the bath rituals I found online due to their excessive requirements for obscure herbs or hand-harvested rose petals, but something did capture my imagination – the idea of using a bath to wash away the spiritual grime as well as the daily grime and kick anything that's no longer working to the kerb.

All I had to do was sprinkle the water with grounding salt (Epsom, Himalayan, sea salt, anything but table salt), soak away, and then visualize any negative energy or stuff I wanted to let go of disappearing down the plughole when I was done (if you don't have a bath you can do the same sort of 'letting go' visualization in a shower – and either use the salt as a scrub or don't worry about it).

Easiest. Visualization. Ever.

I'm not going to lie – it does feel a bit odd waiting it out until the bitter end in an almost empty bath. But let's face it – it's another take on a lie down, so I went with it! And when I stepped out of the tub, I really did feel better: as if I could begin again, free from the tyrannies of self-doubt, procrastination, and wishing I hadn't eaten cereal for lunch.

Everyone feels better after a bath, right? Well, imagine that to the power of ten. Easy, relaxing, and one visualization closer to inner peace – it turns out good vibes are way easier to come by when you chuck the bad ones out with the bath water.

Much like romantic dinners and morning meditation sessions, a ritual bath can only be improved by the addition of a candle or two. And I'm sure you don't need me to tell you that there's something magical about candlelight. The striking of the match, the flicker of the flame, the slow melting of the wax... it's all pretty primal stuff. It was also the obvious starting point for my next everyday ritual.

I'm no stranger to candle magic. When I was a student I had a stash of coloured candles in my room (green for money, blue for protection, orange for success, red for passion) that I'd light, depending on how bad my latest date, seminar or visit to the cashpoint had gone.

There's no shortage of magical rituals you can do with candles, but that wasn't quite what I was looking for here. I wanted something simple and easy that would also make happy use of the stash I had lying around from past birthday and Christmas gifts. Lighting them instead of watching them gather dust seemed like the obvious place to start.

> *I began to use candles to add intention,*
> *purpose and pleasing aromas to*
> *specific moments of time.*

I'd light one while I waited for the kettle to boil in the morning and as the wick caught light, I'd contemplate what I wanted to achieve that day. I put an aromatherapy candle on my desk to light when I needed to really focus on writing a magazine feature. And I dug out a set of wedding-present candlesticks so I could light the box of long tapered candles I'd found in the back of a kitchen cupboard (and add a magical glow to the kids' tea).

We've all made a wish on a birthday candle, right? Well, I decided there was no reason why I couldn't make one *every time* I blew out a candle. Like all the small rituals I'd squeezed into my busy schedule, there was nothing grand or spectacular about this. It was just a quick and easy way to sprinkle a bit of magic on the life I already had. A life that was full and stressful and chaotic; a life that sometimes felt as if it was about to boil over; a life that was crying out for me to live in the moment – moments that a candle or a bath or a cup of tea or a sign from the universe seemed able to provide.

Do it yourself – find magic in the mundane

The premise behind all the routines I turned into rituals in March was ease. I chose elements of my life that I felt I could enhance with minimal effort, hassle or fuss. And that's exactly what I hope you'll do when seeking your own everyday magic. Here are a few other ideas, in case tea, candles and lying in a slowly draining bath don't do it for you!

But first, coffee

Everything I said above about tea, just make it coffee. And maybe make it decaff after the first few, hey?

Natural remedies

Get up in time for the sunrise, make a date with the sunset or try walking barefoot on dew-covered grass. Plant seeds, lie in a field, sunbathe or moon-bathe as you gaze up at the stars. Feed the birds, forage for wild garlic or blackberries, or just get right in there and hug a tree. Simply taking the time to notice the natural world and the passing seasons can be the best magic ritual of all.

Choose a talisman

Pick a piece of jewellery (it can be something you already own or something new) and turn it into a lucky charm by charging it up with your goals or wishes. An easy way to do this is to hold the item in your hands and visualize both yourself and it surrounded by a pure white light. Visualize any negative energy or associations floating away and when it feels right, state your intention, goal or wish out loud three times. Then place the item on a windowsill (or even outside if you're sure it won't be stolen by a passing magpie) on a moonlit night (a full moon is ideal) to soak up some lunar energy and cosmic magic.

Flower power

There's nothing more mood boosting than a bunch of fresh flowers. Take your time arranging a weekly display, choosing flowers and foliage with meanings (yellow roses for friendship, red roses for passion, rosemary for remembrance, snowdrops for hope) that match your intentions. If this feels like a practice you could get into, take a look at the language of flowers in the Victorian era.

Read all about it

Make daily page-turning a non-negotiable. Turn off your phone, block out half an hour and make as many notes as you like in the margins of your book.

Eat me

I mean, we all have to eat! Turn daily sustenance into a ritual by setting a beautiful table (even if it's just for one), stirring good vibes into homemade soup or just taking your time for a change (parsley garnish on the oven chips optional).

Hair & make-up

If you're already spending time on skincare or haircare or make-up application, it doesn't take much to upgrade it to ritual status. There are plenty of products infused with crystals and good vibes out there, but you can just as easily DIY.

Smooth good intentions into your curls, massage in wishes with your moisturizer (use a rose quartz roller for extra good vibes) or paint your nails with colour magic (check out the candle colour magic information in the 'Spiritual supplies' section below for associations that also apply to make-up).

Create an altar

Make a sacred space in your home that you can turn to when you need to refocus, take stock and meditate on what you want out of life – even the smallest of shelves will do. Add crystals, candles, oracle cards, inspiring art or books, items to represent the four elements (earth, air, fire, water), pictures of loved ones, seasonal plants, flowers, beautiful fabric, your vision board or anything else that inspires or feels meaningful to you.

Spiritual supplies

> 'I shop therefore I am.'
> BARBARA KRUGER

It didn't take long for me to run out of candles. And from there it was a swift hop, skip and jump down an internet rabbit hole of mystical potions and soy wax creations in sleek monochrome packaging. It turned out that spiritual shopping had undergone one hell of a glow-up since I'd last looked.

I spent half the 90s trawling sketchy hippie market stalls in my Adidas Gazelles. I still have the wonky blue glass candlesticks and gauzy silk scarves I bought at Granary Wharf in Leeds (known locally as Dark Arches) to set the scene for my bedroom-floor tarot readings. A warren of tiny shops tucked under a huge railway arch, it was the stuff of teenage witch dreams.

I had many favourites among the magical emporiums I found there, but the shop where I bought those candlesticks became a must-visit every time I took the train from my small moorland town to the bright lights of the big city. That said, it wasn't exactly aspirational: imagine the smell of incense smoke mixed with patchouli oil, a rack of cellophane-wrapped yin and yang necklaces and a 'Take Me To Your Dealer' alien poster displayed next to a case of bongs and you've pretty much got the picture.

The good stuff *was* in there (this was where my teenage coven had bought my tarot cards, for starters) but you really had to look for it. And now? Well, I didn't have to fall far down that online rabbit hole to realize that the opposite applied: there was good stuff *everywhere*! And I found myself wanting all of it! Which was a bit of a problem for Best Life Me.

Best Life Me wasn't sure if she should be lusting after crystal-infused pillow mists, handcrafted incense holders or amethyst clusters the size of her head. Best Life Me had designs on making her own moon water under midnight skies and sprinkling homegrown lavender into Kilner jars. Surely she was above having her head turned by shiny, pretty things? And wasn't one of the premises of this year to not blow a small fortune in the name of enlightenment?

Real Life Me wasn't even listening. She needed new candles. She was going in.

I didn't even have to leave the house. Thanks to the internet, and Instagram in particular, you no longer need to live in a hip neighbourhood or a big city or take a special trip to Glastonbury to get your hands on the object of your mystical desires. Give the algorithm a mere whiff of what you're after and you'll find yourself bombarded by crystal dealers, herbalists, artisan makers and chic lifestyle stores filled with magical tinctures and potions.

Once I started looking, I wanted it all. I wanted small batch flower essences created by a folk herbalist called Roberta in the depths of the Cotswolds countryside. I wanted beautifully packaged candles scented with essential oils and poured in a protective circle by a witch named Semra. I wanted crystal-infused aura spray made under the full moon by Paolo, a Sardinian reflexologist to the stars. I wanted crystals so desirable they sold out the second they were posted on Instagram. I wanted trinkets and talismans and bundles of herbs tied up with clear quartz and twine. I wanted to fill my life with magic potions and bad-vibe-banishing moon mists.

And if I could do it while supporting small spiritual businesses at the same time, was that really so bad? The more I thought about it the more I felt that it couldn't possibly be. I decided there must be a compromise to be found between Best Life Me's self-righteous grow-your-own vibes and the very Real Life Me double tapping every scented candle on Instagram.

That compromise, I concluded, was shopping small, making an effort to know who I was buying from, and trying to be as sustainable in my choices as possible. After all, every mystical thinker needs a few choice items in their toolkit – candles, essential oils, a crystal or two. I decided I was going to create a perfect example: nothing excessive, nothing too fancy, just a selection of carefully sourced, beautiful things to add even more magic to my day-to-day.

Fancy creating your own mystical toolkit? You know those lists you find at the start of cookbooks, detailing the essentials you should stock your pantry with before you even think about setting foot in the kitchen? Think of what follows as one of those, with added rose quartz.

Do it yourself – mystical toolkit #1

Here's my toolkit of magical must-haves. Do take the term 'must-have' with an appropriate pinch of (grounding) salt, though. There's nothing you absolutely have to buy to live a mystical life – however, if you're so inclined, some things are nice to have. *For more recommendations, and some of my favourite shops and brands, check out the March entry in the Spiritual Sourcebook at the back of the book.*

Candles

Every mystical toolkit needs a stash of candles. However, there's no need to spend a lot of money on them unless you want to. Plain pillar and table candles (in a variety of colours if you fancy getting into some colour magic) will totally do the trick.

Candle colour magic

Light a candle in a hue that corresponds with what you're looking to bring into your life for some easy magic (see below). You can also apply the principles of colour magic to make-up, nail varnish, clothes, interior lighting, whatever you like!

Black – Psychic protection, banishing bad vibes, accepting endings

White – Peace, serenity, truth, hope

Red – Energy, passion, seduction, sex, courage

Orange – Confidence, creativity, great ideas

Yellow – Joy, happiness, focus, friendship, communication, travel

Green – Money, health, luck, fertility, healing

Blue – Peace, understanding, truth, hope, honesty

Purple – Intuition, spirituality, beating addiction, getting in touch with your higher self

Pink – Love, self-love, romance, beauty, kindness, healing

Brown – Stability, grounding, strength, a positive work ethic

Silver – Money, feminine energy, healing, inner peace, dreams, moon power

Gold – Money, masculine energy, fame, fortune, sun power

Aura sprays

There's no easier way to banish bad vibes than with a spritz of aura spray (a scented mist that's said to help protect and clear a person's space or aura). These potions can also be used to cleanse crystals, seal intentions and up the magic on manifestation (get that vision board coated in a fragrant fine mist immediately).

There are all sorts of different blends available, often infused with crystals or moonlight or reiki energy or all three. Try using one to reset your space at the end of a stressful day, to power back up after a tricky conversation, or to keep vibes high on the go (stash a bottle in your bag for spiritual emergencies). I also like using mine to send important messages, emails or pitches out into the world doused in positivity (a light mist over the laptop might not be Apple-approved but it works every time for me). *Check out the March entry in the Spiritual Sourcebook for recommendations.*

Incense and essential oils

I'm pretty sure that we all understand the transportive power of fragrance. And by that I don't mean the fleeting hope that your life might be transformed into Keira Knightley's with a spritz of Chanel's Coco Mademoiselle.

I mean that heady mix of lavender soap and greenhouse tomatoes that takes you straight back to long summer holidays spent at your grandparents' house. Or the exact combination of salty air and suntan lotion that transports you to days spent gazing at a holiday horizon. Or the fast track to Christmas spirit served up by clementines and cinnamon. There's magic galore in scent, which makes it another ideal addition to the mystical toolkit.

I've long been a fan of incense – there's something mesmerizing about watching its plumes of smoke unfurl – but for pure aromatics there's nothing quite like an essential oil diffuser. I was given a plug-in one for Christmas a few years back and it's turned out to be one of my favourite gifts ever.

Whichever tools or method you choose, fragrance can be used to create atmosphere, carve out peaceful moments or add aromatic reminders to tune in, relax or stay on track. Try lavender for comfort and relaxation, peppermint for concentration and focus, orange for positive vibes, or eucalyptus for clearing the air. Begin to build your own stash of essential oils and you'll soon have a scented solution to everything life throws your way.

Smoke & herbs

There are all sorts of ways to use herbs in magical ritual (rose for love, thyme for strength, lavender for sleep), but I found myself most drawn to the idea of using herbal smoke offerings to clear, cleanse and invite in positive energy.

My Instagram feed was full of it, too. Impossibly cool people in impossibly cool kitchens using bundles of sage to 'smudge' their spaces in pursuit of #goodvibesonly. It reminded me of the cinnamon sticks I used to burn for magical good fortune in my 90s attic bedroom or the incense smoke that unfurled over all my teenage-witch tarot readings.

I soon discovered, though, that smudging has cultural appropriation issues. I found an article online about the harmful co-opting and commercialization of this Native American ceremonial practice – one that was illegal, along with practising other aspects of First Nations religion or culture, until the American Indian Religious Freedom Act of 1978 – and the resulting over-harvesting of white sage.

It sounded like the opposite of high vibe to me. Even worse, in my haste to join the Insta-crowd I'd already ordered an aesthetically pleasing bundle of herbs from a ranch in Colorado in the US. It had been made using blue sage rather than white but I still felt pretty uncomfortable about lighting it. I started eyeing up the ethically harvested palo santo (a fragrant sacred wood that can be used in a similar way to herbs) I'd recently been given by a friend and wondered if that was problematic too. Should I just stick to candles and incense? Was there a less harmful way to use smoke and herbs?

It's a sensitive subject, but if you opt to use locally sourced herbs and make an effort to align your rituals and language with practices more closely associated with your own culture (burning incense/herbs and using smoke is common to many cultural traditions and religions), I don't think smoke cleansing in itself is a no-no. It just requires a bit of sensitivity and consideration.

You could try drying and tying your own magical creations, or seek out makers crafting herbal bundles based on traditions connected to your personal heritage. You could take the witchcraft route and burn small amounts of herbs using a charcoal disc and a heatproof bowl. You could use stuff you already have lying around the house and the contents of your kitchen cupboards, combined with some thought, research and respect for the practices and traditions of other cultures.

Basically, just don't autopilot straight to the imported white sage! And if you do decide to use it try to ask questions about its harvesting, ethics and any profit distribution.

Whichever tools you choose, a smoke cleansing or offering usually involves lighting your herbs/incense and then allowing the smoke to billow into every corner of your space. Open a window so that any negative energy can be released and repeat your intentions aloud as you visualize bad vibes making a hasty exit along with the smoke.

Crystals

You can skip ahead to the 'Get stoned' section in the July chapter for more insight into crystals, but in March I was satisfied with the idea that the best way to pick a crystal is to simply go for the one you think is the prettiest. I also have a tendency to like anything if it's about to sell out, which is how I ended up adding a beautiful green moonstone sphere to my virtual basket in a spiritual shopping panic one evening. It was a pretty big one, but size really doesn't matter where crystals are concerned.

If you don't know where to start or what to pick, you can't go wrong with a handful of starter-sized tumblestones: rose quartz for love, citrine for positive energy, and amethyst to big up your psychic powers. Slip one into your bag, your desk drawer or under your pillow for a bit of extra help where you need it most.

Bath salts

If you're going to get in there with the ritual baths you'll need a serious salt stash in your mystical toolkit. There are all sorts of beautifully packaged aromatic salt bath blends out there but you can also use ordinary Epsom salts (otherwise known as magnesium sulfate, and available from most chemists), sea salt or pink Himalayan salt. Mix up your own salt blend, add a few drops of essential oil (lavender is my fave) and you're good to go.

Books

I've mentioned my teetering stack of mystical books a few times, and you'll find those and more recommendations in the 'Read all about it' sections in the Spiritual Sourcebook. Inspo galore for a stack of your own.

April

IT'S JUST
A (MOON) PHASE

Celebration: Earth Day

Moon: Pink moon

Sign: Aries

Crystal: Clear quartz

Element: Fire

Tarot: The Emperor

By the light of the moon

'Just like the moon. your greatest magic will
come in times of darkness when you have
no choice but to trust your own power.'

JILL WINTERSTEEN

Ever had a New Year's resolution last beyond January? I hadn't.
So, getting all the way to Easter Sunday (1 April 2018) with my
mystical mission felt like something to celebrate. It was the
perfect long weekend for it, too.

You just know there's a 'but' coming, right?

Yep, turned out life hadn't quite got the memo. I spent that Easter
Sunday vacuuming up piles of brick dust (created by the builders)
in the basement and feeling sick every time I looked at Instagram.
Which I was doing obsessively. I might have found a way to keep
the magic alive through the busiest March of my life, but while I
was muttering wishes into my tea, it seemed everyone else had
made long-weekend plans without me.

Ever been there? Then you'll know both the sinking feeling and
the hot shame that goes with the territory. I hadn't felt like this
in my adult life before. And I'd never imagined I was the kind of
person who'd get worked up about being missed off a few invite
lists. And yet here I was all the same. I didn't understand it.

I tried to keep my mind occupied. I reorganized storage boxes. I
shifted the unused wedding-present fondue set from one shelf to
another. I told myself I didn't care about drinking rosé in expensive
gastropubs or sharing grazing platters over new kitchen islands,

but I did. Banker-belt imposter syndrome was alive and well. And I hated myself for engaging with it.

Why did I even want a seat at this particular table? Why was I so desperate to belong to a world that felt so alien to me? Tears fell hard and fast as I washed the brick dust off in the shower that evening. Does no one like me? Will I ever fit in? Why do I feel like I've regressed a couple of decades? Where the hell are my people? My bad-vibes plughole had its work cut out that night.

But then the universe threw me a line. As I popped outside to retrieve a lost toy from the garden I saw the moon – big, bright and beautiful – peek through a gap in a cloud-covered sky. It felt like exactly the right omen at exactly the right time. And as I gazed up, I knew instantly what my plan for April should be.

I'd just started reading Yasmin Boland's *Moonology* guide and was busy obsessing over online moon-phase calendars and the wax and wane of the moon cycle. I hadn't paid this much attention to the night sky since I was a teenager, and it was all beginning to come back to me. I found myself remembering the witchy wise woman in a crystal shop in Leeds who told my 14-year-old self she should always make a wish on the crescent moon. And I remembered the magical feeling I'd get when the full moon lit up the otherwise pitch-black track from the street to my house in the Yorkshire countryside – like it was shining just for me. I was back in the game.

I knew now, for example, that although my 1 April good omen moon looked full, it was actually just beginning to wane – the aftermath of the 31 March full moon in Libra, which was a blue moon on account of it being the second full moon that month.

I knew that full moons were great for wishes coming true and feeling feelings and getting real about what needs to go in your life. And I'd learnt that the waning phase I was seeing now was all about taking stock, letting go, gathering strength and getting ready to hit the ground running when the moon became new again.

As for new moons, well, if they were for fresh starts and setting intentions and believing in better things ahead, I was definitely in. A mini New Year's every single month – why hadn't someone told me about that before?

Just in case I lost you at 'blue moon' there, let's backtrack a bit.

 You really don't need to be mystically minded to harness the power of the moon.

Who hasn't basked in the glow of a full moon on the way home from a great night out? Or watched it rise like magic over a festival stage? Or sat awestruck on a balmy dark moon evening beneath a sky full of twinkling stars?

There's something otherworldly and magical about gazing up at the night sky, which is why earthlings have been trying to get to grips with the mysteries of the moon for millennia. You don't need me or anyone else to tell you that the moon is magical. You already know it. And it's right there in the sky above to remind you, should you ever forget. Harnessing the power of the moon's different phases to make positive changes in your life is just the next obvious step.

That's what I decided, anyway. I'd reached a point where rather than waste energy agonizing over which mystical practice I should explore next, I just assumed that whatever was appearing on my radar was meant to be. And right then, the moon was everywhere. It was all over my Instagram feed, on the trinket tray a friend gave me as a belated birthday gift, in the books by my bedside, and in the night-sky backdrops of every poignant movie scene I attempted to distract myself with on Netflix.

Soon it was in my email inbox, too. I'd been following the American artist and spiritual teacher Alexandra Roxo's Instagram with fascination, so when she offered up the chance to join one of her monthly new-moon rituals for free (normally part of a paid membership group called Moon Club she ran with Ruby Warrington from astro site The Numinous), I knew I had to do it.

That didn't mean I wasn't slightly terrified by the idea of joining an online ritual with a load of people who were already part of a moon-worshipping members' club, though. Not that I was going to let that stop me. I registered for the Zoom meeting, clicked the right link at the right time and gave my children unrestricted iPad access for the duration. I was going in.

And that's how I found myself, two weeks after that miserable Easter Sunday, having the most magical experience in the most ordinary surroundings (there's nothing like sitting on your bed next to a massive pile of laundry to keep things real). And it wasn't just the moon that made it magical, either – it was those moon-worshippers I'd been so nervous about meeting online. Here were all these other people, connected via the power of the internet, logged in from wherever they were in the world, for the same reason, at the same moment in time. It was amazing.

And there were so many of them. The chat box filled with hellos from California to Cape Town and Bristol to Brazil. I really wasn't the only person out there interested in this stuff! Here were over a hundred people (my kind of people!) tuned in to listen to a red-clad, red-haired Alexandra Roxo wax lyrical about the power of storytelling and the importance of community and the magic of the new moon. I was mesmerized.

Earlier that week we'd been sent an email explaining that the theme of the new-moon ritual was 'Fuel to the Fire' – a guided visualization journey to help us own our stories and use our voices as a force for change. So far so good. There was also a list of things we might want to do to up the positive vibes during the ritual, such as using crystals or lighting candles. I'd totally forgotten about that part so I quickly snuck out of my bedroom to find my green moonstone, keeping an ear out for squabbling sisters on the way. And then we dived in.

It was all so brilliantly simple. Most of my mystical adventures so far had taken place outside my house, after much negotiating with children and babysitters. But here I was, eye mask to hand, headphones plugged in, only half wondering if I should check on the kids one last time. I forced myself to focus as Alexandra began playing a drum beat and guided us to go down, down, down, down, down, down, down. I'd never entered a meditative state or another world quite so quickly before.

Soon I found myself visualizing a map of the world covered in tiny, bright, star-like dots, each one representing another soul tuned in to this journey with me. I really could feel the power of that connection, that shared experience reaching out through cyberspace and headphones into the here and now.

The journey took us into a sacred space where we were asked to invite in our guides and ancestors. I soon assembled quite the cast. My elephant was there, a strong and silent figure in the background. My grandad was there too, which was the best feeling ever. He'd died just a couple of weeks earlier and we hadn't yet had the funeral.

Then I realized that my late father-in-law was also there, as was a guy called Andy I'd worked with at *Time* magazine more than a decade earlier. I found myself feeling distracted. Surely I should be calling in angels or plant spirits or magical beings, not the guest list for the world's most awkward drinks party. Without any drinks! Still, I presumed my mind was conjuring this strange scenario for a reason and I went with it.

I found myself walking among these guides, trying my best to tune in and receive some sort of message from them. But it wasn't working. I couldn't hear a thing. What I *could* hear was a quiet but clear voice that seemed to be coming from deep within me. It was telling me to carry on, to keep going and to stop worrying about what other people think (ancestral guides included, apparently).

The thing was, it felt like the truth. I knew I was a shapeshifter and a people-pleaser. I couldn't remember a time when I hadn't been desperate for people to like me. In my first year at university, I became known for my ability to be all things to all people. I was in with the cool girls and the alt girls and the club kids and the public-school boys who'd taken a wrong turn on their path to Oxford or Edinburgh.

If someone liked me, I invariably liked them back, without question. And then I made myself in their image. You think I'm cool? I'll be cool. You think I like techno? I'll dance to that repetitive beat like no one's watching. You think your mother would like me? Sure, I can dress for high tea at the country pile.

I didn't really think about who I was or what I liked or what mattered to me. I just did what I could to make people like me and basked in the warm glow that was reflected back. I was good at it, too.

Of course, those first few terms at university or college, or the early weeks in a first job, are prime for an identity crisis and for most people (me included) things eventually get better. By the summer of that first university year I'd found my people, my forever friends: the seven girls who have stood by me through every high and all the lows since. And yet I still find myself craving the approval of others. And I still find it difficult to locate my own opinion on something.

The journalist in me likes to see multiple sides to every story, and I research everything to excess. I'll often find myself checking what *The Guardian* or *Vogue* think about a film I've seen or a book I've read before I decide what *I* think. I'm terrified of upsetting people or offending people or getting it wrong. It remains impossible for me to celebrate a birthday or throw a party without the guest list spiralling out of control within seconds. I can't leave anyone out. I must not offend. I must be liked. Table for everyone I've ever met at 8 p.m. this Saturday?

If this sounds ridiculous, that's because it is. But I know I'm not the only one who feels the need to mould myself in order to fit in. How many of us find validation in other people's approval? Friends, family, lovers: please like me; please believe in me; please make me feel like I belong.

I knew that voice within me was right. I wasn't sure if I was even following Alexandra's visualization anymore – I was on my own path, doing my own thing, making sense of something I hoped would translate in the real world. I felt instantly lighter, and as if I had a hell of a lot of work to do at the same time.

I knew what my new-moon intentions had to be. I knew I needed to own my own story. I knew I needed to stop trying so hard to become what I thought the world wanted me to be. I needed to become myself. I needed to remember the words of wisdom that had kicked off this whole mystical year: *If you lose your way in life, look back to what lit you up when you were younger.* It was time to stop caring about what other people thought of me and become my truest self.

As the journey ended and Alexandra talked us slowly back into the room I felt brave enough to do something I'd never done before: I told the truth (in a Zoom chat box). I wrote that I'd defined myself by other people's opinions for way too long. That my self-worth was completely and utterly tied up in whether or not people liked me or thought I was a 'good' person. And that becoming who I really am, without hesitation, was my 'Fuel to the Fire'.

That Zoom chat box was soon filled with other people doing exactly the same thing. Showing up, speaking the truth, sharing their voices, setting intentions to do what they love, follow dreams and make a difference in the world. I'd never witnessed so much honesty and vulnerability in action in one place before. I was awestruck. Maybe we really are all the same underneath. I wasn't the only person struggling to find her purpose or live life on her own terms. Maybe it's the same for everyone. Even the visions of perfection I like to hate-follow on Instagram.

 ✧ That night I slept with my new-moon intentions under my pillow, and I felt more powered up and ready for change than ever before.

I loved the idea that a new moon could give me this opportunity for renewal every single month. Suddenly, making New Year's resolutions felt so amateurish. Why put all your eggs in that cold

January basket when you have the option of a brand new start every 29.5 days? I was totally sold.

Living my life attuned to the moon made perfect sense. Life happens in cycles, after all. And we're all constantly changing and evolving. Sometimes we're up; sometimes we're down. Sometimes we feel full, glowing and powerful; sometimes we just need to start over. Sometimes we're ready to make stuff happen and other times we need to press pause and gather strength. I loved the idea that whatever life was throwing at me, the moon had a phase for it. And it was right there in the sky above, ready to show me the way.

Just a few days after that online ritual I found myself making a wish on the first sliver of a waxing crescent moon for the first time in decades. It was the night of my grandad's funeral and I'd never needed magic more. Ten days after that I wrote a manifestation missive to charge with my crystals under the full moon. And a list of everything I was ready to let go of to make space for those dreams to come true. When that full moon began to wane I allowed myself some breathing space, slowed down and said no more often, safe in the knowledge that the fresh energy of the new moon would soon fire things up again.

I liked living with this gentle ebb and flow. I liked that it was all so easy. I didn't have to be organized or to plan anything or even to have any spare time. All I had to do was look up, soak it all in and let nature and magic and the night sky lead the way.

It made a difference, too. I stopped trying to keep up and started trying to move forwards. I powered ahead when the time was right and gave myself a break when I needed to. I no longer felt the need to be always on it and making stuff happen. I did what I could and I started where I was.

I began to make choices that felt right because they *were* right, rather than overthinking outcomes that might never happen until I was paralyzed by indecision. My life didn't suddenly become perfect, and I wasn't getting it right all the time, but the beginnings of a natural flow started to emerge.

I moved heaven and earth to head home to Yorkshire when my friend Louise flew back from the US to visit her family in our mutual hometown. I booked nights out in London with my university friends. I began to pay attention to how I felt when I was with certain people and stopped trying to make plans with anyone who left me feeling drained or not good enough.

I set up WhatsApp groups with friends I hadn't spoken to for a while. I stopped caring so much if I wasn't invited to something. I looked for more online rituals and sought out new groups of like-minded souls. I reached out to people on Instagram. I started feeling like myself again. I began to find my people. I picked up the invitation to my childhood friend Jane's wedding in Byron Bay, Australia, which had been pinned to the fridge for weeks, and I dared to ask myself why I couldn't be there to celebrate her big day.

The more I tuned in to the moon cycle and thought about how I really felt and what I really wanted out of life, the more my mindset changed. The more my mindset changed, the more life felt full of potential. The more life felt full of potential, the happier I became. The happier I became, the easier it was to connect with other people, take risks and believe that the universe really did have my back.

The moon is magic.

Do it yourself – attune to the moon

If you're interested in diving into moon magic in more detail there are some brilliant books out there (see the April entry of the Sourcebook for my recommendations). Below is a simplified rundown of the main phases of the moon cycle to get you started. It's what works for me, what sparks my imagination, and a framework for harnessing the power of the moon that I have found easy to incorporate into my life.

New moon

What is it? This is the beginning of the moon cycle. The alignment of the Earth, the sun and the moon leaves the side of the moon that faces our planet in darkness, so it's not visible. It's the best time of the month to see the stars!

When can you see it? You can't. However, in magical practice the very first sliver of the waxing crescent moon (see below) is sometimes treated as the new moon – and that you definitely can see. I love setting intentions in the darkness of the new moon, but I always save an extra wish for the moment I first see the waxing crescent.

What does it mean? Think of the new moon as a fresh start, a clean slate or a blank page. This is thought to be the best time to set intentions and define goals for the future... that mini monthly New Year!

How do I harness its power? There's no right or wrong way to harness the power of the new moon. You might want to join a new-moon ritual online or in person, or simply take some time out to look within, to meditate, or to freewrite your ideas on what you want to bring forth in this new cycle. A home ritual can be as simple as lighting a candle and writing down your intentions on the night of the new moon.

Waxing moon

What is it? The phase that falls between the new and full moon sees the moon's illumination grow gradually. A slim crescent moon brightens to reveal the first quarter (you might call this a half moon) around seven days after the new moon and then a waxing gibbous moon as it becomes full again.

When can I see it? On a clear night, the first crescent can usually be seen shortly after sunset a few days after the new moon. When the waxing moon is almost full you might spot it in the afternoon or early evening as well as in the night sky.

What does it mean? The waxing stage of the moon cycle is said to be a period of high energy and power. Now is the time to focus on and really work towards your goals, to embrace progress, and if the mood takes you, to try something new.

How do I harness its power? Keep checking in with yourself and your plans during this part of the moon cycle. Now is the best time to make things happen and be productive, so stay focused, repeat your intentions to yourself and don't shy away from taking steps towards whatever your heart desires. You might want to relight that new moon candle or refocus your energy with a ritual bath.

Full moon

What is it? Bright, bold and lighting up the sky, this is the big one. The full moon occurs around 14 days after the new moon.

When can I see it? All night long, provided the clouds play ball.

What does it mean? There's so much folklore around the full moon that even the most scathing cynics tend to be willing to acknowledge its ability to make life feel more intense. The power of the full moon makes it the ideal time to reflect on how you've grown and what you've achieved since the new moon a fortnight ago.

Full moon can be a powerful time for manifestation and wishes coming true, too. I like to think of it as a magical double whammy. It's the cumulative, power-packed final fling of the moon's waxing 'growth' phase; however, because it also spells the beginning of the waning 'release' phase, it's a time to be honest about what you need to let go of, too. The full moon is thought to be the perfect time to wave goodbye to bad vibes, negativity and anything you want to kick to the kerb.

How do I harness its power? To make the most of the full moon all you really have to do is get outside and bathe in its light. Or at least open your bedroom curtains a bit to let that light shine in. You can also charge your crystals, keep your eyes peeled for magical big reveals, or write down everything you want to let go of on a piece of paper and burn it to ash.

Waning moon

What is it? In this phase the moon's visible illumination begins to reduce – just a little at first, to a waning gibbous moon, then to its third quarter (around seven days after the full moon) and finally to a sliver of waning crescent before the new moon.

When can I see it? The waning gibbous moon is visible late at night and also in the early-morning sky before it sets. The last quarter is another moon you might spot in the morning, but as the moon wanes towards its final crescent it's best seen just before dawn. And as the moon moves into its dark phase and gradually becomes new again, it's not visible at all.

What does it mean? The waning moon is said to be the best time to press pause, look within and be honest about what really matters to us. It's a time of release and relief, in preparation for the next cycle. A time to be honest about what's working for you and what really isn't. So, round up those negative thoughts and limiting beliefs and that voice in your head that tells you you're not good enough, and send it all packing.

How do I harness its power? Allow yourself some space and time to take stock. Now is a great time for meditation, visualization and saying no to anything that doesn't light you up. Become at one with your sofa, restore your energy and just allow yourself to *be*, because before you know it the new moon will return and the cycle will begin all over again.

May

DON'T HATE. MEDITATE

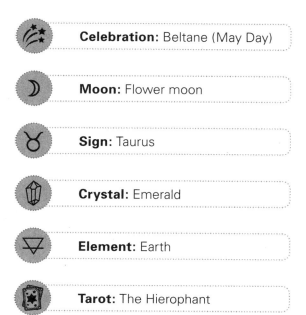

Celebration: Beltane (May Day)

Moon: Flower moon

Sign: Taurus

Crystal: Emerald

Element: Earth

Tarot: The Hierophant

Meditation nation

'Be here now. Be someplace else
later. Is that so complicated?'
DAVID M. BADER

Once I'd decided to spend more time looking within, there was only one direction that May could go. And if you've ever spent *shavasana* (the meditative pose at the end of yoga) coming up with the perfect 'last word' you *wish* you'd had in an argument a decade ago, we're probably starting from a similar page where meditation is concerned.

Likewise, if you've ever read a Sunday supplement feature about the secret of someone's success and found your intrigue turn to despair when their big reveal is a stoical commitment to daily meditation, I get it. I mean, couldn't it be something else, just this once – something a bit less quiet and still and suspiciously straightforward?

What do these glowing, contemplative types *do* with all their thoughts? And how can something that sounds so easy (and potentially life-changing) be so difficult to get on board with? It isn't just me, is it? Consider this chapter a safe space for the meditatively challenged. Been there, done that, got distracted.

None of which changes the fact that meditation is having a moment. The last few years have seen a proliferation of techy meditation and mindfulness tools. You can't fail to have noticed all the apps (Headspace and Calm being two of the UK's best known), YouTube channels and Transcendental Meditation ads that pop up on Instagram while you're quietly stalking other people's lunch choices.

You might be all over it, headphones in and good to go, or you might be up in arms about the commodification of a practice that's as old as the Vedas (early Sanskrit scriptures). Regardless, meditation has gone mainstream. And this is no bad thing.

> *There's a growing body of evidence that meditation has a positive impact on anxiety, depression, blood pressure and more.*

Meditation as a spiritual and religious practice dates back thousands of years but its arrival in the West, particularly as the more secular practice we know today, is very much a 20th-century affair. Yet discovering the benefits of meditation is no longer the preserve of well-connected global superstars (like The Beatles studying with Maharishi in 1968) or hippie-trail early adopters – it's all there, ready and waiting, on your phone!

It probably won't surprise you to hear that meditation and I have history. Remember my worldly rollerblading Freshers' Week crush – the one I tried to impress by getting into yoga? He was also into meditation. Not that this meant he managed to explain it to me in a way that made any sense. I had to find myself another tie-dye-clad globetrotter (there were a lot of them about in 1996) in the university bar to offer up some tips I could actually put to use. Soon, I was equipped with some (possibly dubious) instructions and a beer mat scrawled with the words *Om Shanti*.

It all *sounded* so easy: sit quietly, close your eyes and silently repeat this mantra (which invokes universal peace) over and over, returning to it whenever a stray thought arises. In reality, it went a little like this:

'*Om Shanti, Om Shanti, Om...* What should I wear tonight? *Om Shanti...* Did I miss another essay deadline? *Om Shanti, Om Shanti, Shanti...* Should I try a different mantra? *Om...* Bit hungry. Tired. Bored. Dead leg. *Shanti, Shanti, Shanti...* Best check the time... Was that the phone ringing?'

So far so normal, right? We have up to 50 thoughts a minute, so it's pretty much impossible to empty our heads of them completely. In fact, a more professional meditation teacher (many years later) told me that the point of meditation is to achieve an absence of desire and that no one is *ever* capable of that for more than a few seconds.

But, back to the 90s and my attempts to locate stillness on a hard single bed in a tiny university accommodation room...

I'd like you to imagine something more glamorous, but I'm almost certainly wearing the cream towelling dressing gown my mum bought me from Marks & Spencer in Leeds before we drove an overstuffed Ford Ka down the M62. In terms of décor, there's definitely a serious floor-drobe situation going on. I may or may not have just stubbed out a Marlboro Light. Beverage options of the era include a pink plastic cup of vodka mixed with neat lemon squash, strong tea sprinkled with powdered milk or, on push-the-boat-out special occasions, a mushroom cup-a-soup.

It's either sweltering because the communal heating's just come on or freezing cold (for the other 23 hours of the day). You can probably hear the last bars of Oasis's 'Wonderwall' playing out in the distance somewhere. Or smell the incense that's dropping ash over an unfinished essay.

Maybe you can even imagine the moment when for just a few minutes, I actually manage to stick with that mantra for the very first time. The thoughts are still there of course, but I let them pass on by. I don't let them distract me. I breathe deeply. I tune in. I sink into myself. I actually do it. And you know what, it's amazing when the noise stops.

Those few minutes turned out to be enough to pique my interest in what might be if I managed to make meditation part of my life. I started to really tune in during *shavasana*, and I began to notice the benefits of learning how to go beyond the surface chatter of my mind. I wasn't a regular, dedicated meditator but it became something I could turn to when I needed to locate some inner peace.

That on-again-off-again practice was it for a while, until Headspace launched its app in 2012. As a stressed-out freelance writer and weekday single parent (my husband was working in London while I held the fort in Bristol) to a baby and a pre-schooler, I was a shoo-in for a download that promised a shortcut to clarity. I'd get the kids to bed then lie down with my phone by my side, often falling asleep well before the end of the recording. I don't know whether that meant I didn't get everything I should have out of it – with two children under four, sleep was a goal in itself – but from then on, meditation became a more regular part of my survival toolkit.

I've turned to meditation in various forms (silent, guided, on the other end of an app) and mindfulness (which is a form of meditation) whenever I've felt overwhelmed by life and the whirring To Do list in my head. I've meditated on planes, in traffic jams and in dentists' chairs. Although I was wary of ideas about meditation as a corporate productivity tool, I knew that as a way to tune in, chill out and hear my inner voice over the noise, it worked for me.

So why on earth wasn't it something I was doing daily in the here and now? This, of course, became my plan for May, and not just because #*meditationmay* had a certain ring to it.

It was already shaping up to be a challenging month. Something wasn't right at the head office of the magazine I was working for. I was used to getting messages from freelance writers who hadn't been paid on time by the accounts department, but now regulars like myself and my fellow editors were being fobbed off with emails about delays in the system. It felt ominous, like the beginning of the end. And while I waited to discover if my hunch was right, I definitely needed a distraction.

I didn't set any rules for Meditation May, other than I had to meditate for at least five minutes every day – no bunking off. I was excited to see whether making meditation a regular rather than random part of my life would make a difference. And I was totally up for becoming glowing and successful and one day revealing all in a smug magazine interview.

Of course, there was one glaring flaw in the plan: I'd actually have to do it. Five minutes a day sounds like nothing. Five minutes a day *is* nothing (especially when those five minutes result in you feeling better than you did five minutes earlier). But, just like going to the gym, putting away laundry and grand plans to batch cook like a domestic goddess, it's somehow easier said than done.

I decided to throw everything I had at meditation. Everything and anything I could think of that might make it more fun and easier to stick to. I tried getting up early, lighting a scented candle and enjoying the stillness of the morning... until my peace-shattering seven-year-old made it clear that her enjoyment of morning stillness would never be complete without me pouring her Cheerios.

I considered signing up for a local class or one of the 'Introduction to Transcendental Meditation' talks that kept stalking me on Instagram. I even considered going back to the Headspace app, but somehow that didn't feel right either. I really wanted to do it on my own.

I wanted to prove to myself that meditation is free and available to anyone who makes time for it.

I wanted to show that anyone can benefit from it, wherever and whoever they are. If there was ever a mystical adventure that had no place in my direct debits, surely this was it.

In the end, it was my love of a good lie down that sorted it. I started finding beautifully worded guided meditations on YouTube and dedicating my lunch break to lying on my bed, plugged in and ready to dive deep. Once I got into it, I couldn't get enough. And I was doing way more than five minutes! I was being transformed in a desert oasis. I was filling my body with light. I was travelling through a tunnel to meet my spirit guide. I was opening my heart like an unfurling rose. It was all infinitely more compelling than heating up soup and checking out my online supermarket order.

It might sound as if I had it nailed in the first few days, but as the month went on it became a problem. I'd found my 'thing', a way to meditate every day that was enjoyable and relaxing and truly took me out of myself and into another world. The trouble was, I liked it a bit too much. I found myself pressing play on longer and longer sessions. I couldn't get past breakfast without starting to contemplate which visualization I'd do later that day. I started declaring it lunchtime earlier and earlier

I was convinced that any day now I'd receive some sort of download from the cosmos that would change my life forever, if only I remained horizontal. In a laughable turn of events, I'd become addicted to meditation.

My friend Lizzy saw right through it. She'd called to offer me a commission, writing about a new Spice Girls exhibition, and a ticket to see Bjork with her later that month.

'So, what you're telling me is that you think you're about to lose your job at *Smallish* [the magazine I was working for]?' Lizzy said.

'Probably,' I replied. 'Actually, yes. I don't think I'll see another penny from them.'

'And you're dealing with this by lying on your bed for hours imagining you're in Middle-earth?'

'Erm...'

'You need to stop that. Now.'

It was a wake-up call. I knew deep down that my guided meditation obsession meant I was not only avoiding having to think about what was happening with my job but also avoiding ever having to truly calm my mind. It's great fun being guided through subterranean worlds and unwrapping imaginary gifts from the universe, but I knew what I really needed from my meditation practice was to tune in to myself more. And it would be altogether more practical if it didn't require an hour of listening to someone else's voice for me to achieve that.

So for the second half of May, I forced myself to remain seated during meditation. And I went back to the mantra. And sometimes I just concentrated on my breathing, using some of the techniques

I'd learnt through yoga. I set myself a timer for five minutes and I did it till it was done. One step at a time, one day at a time, five minutes at a time.

When Lizzy and I went to that Bjork gig there was magic in the air. The moon was nearly at its first quarter and it felt like something was building. We watched as lightning cracked right over the stage. It wasn't a rainbow, but it felt like a sign. A new beginning. And that new beginning felt a lot like not worrying about the direction the world was about to take me in.

Maybe my magazine job was about to be no more. Maybe it wasn't. Maybe I'd find a way to make things work, either way. I wondered if this was what it meant to trust the universe. I wondered if this was what my month of meditation was leading me towards.

Meditation is a practice and it *takes* practice, but as the month drew to a close I knew that the only thing that had ever got in my way was me. No matter how much I wanted to blame my lack of commitment to meditation on motherhood or work or the laundry mountain at the top of the stairs, it was always me.

And even though I'd set myself a meditation goal for the month, I could see now that this wasn't about an achievement or ticking a neat spiritual rite-of-passage box. I came to see meditation as a muscle I needed to flex. The more I did it, the easier it was and the more difficult it became to believe my own lame excuses. Spoiler: we've *all* got five minutes.

Once I got over myself, I got into myself in the best possible way. I felt calmer. I felt clearer. My mind was no longer under attack from mental notes about checking tyre pressures or buying car insurance every time I closed my eyes. And this was just the beginning. By the end of May I was extending my sessions by a few minutes each time. I felt that I had a tool I could easily use to calm myself down in any stressful situation. I also found I could use meditation to really tune in to myself and find the answers to questions my indecisive mind would otherwise struggle with.

I meditated my way to a decision – to stop working for the magazine that was no longer paying my invoices on time; or paying them at all, in fact. And no matter how much they protested and promised that they'd sort their accounts by the end of the week, I stuck to my guns. I decided to start knowing my worth and putting myself first. And it felt good.

And on one particularly bold day, right at the end of May, I made a decision to put a flight to my friend's wedding in Australia on my credit card. Just. Like. That. I felt like a different person. Bolder. Braver. Reckless, but in a good way.

Meditation wasn't just a tick-box tool – it was a game-changer. A game-changer that gave me the power to tune in and know whether something felt right or not. A game-changer that really was free and easy and available to anyone, anytime. A Mystical Thinking holy grail.

Do it yourself – find your path to meditation

There's no wrong or right way to meditate – it's all about finding what works for you. And this is definitely one mystical adventure where the journey is more important than the destination. In fact, the journey *is* the destination. Check out these suggestions for calming your mind, five minutes at a time.

Try out an app

Both Calm and Headspace have free meditation content.

Check out YouTube

I spent a lot of time in the first half of May listening to 'Meditations By Rasa' on YouTube and they are wonderful. There are plenty of other channels on there too, though. See which ones you feel intuitively drawn to and give them a go.

Attend a class

Sometimes the easiest way to focus is to put someone else in charge. Check out your local yoga studio to see if they run meditation classes. Or, if you're lucky enough to have one near you, try a course at a meditation centre. You'll find more recommendations in the May entry in the Spiritual Sourcebook.

Just breathe

Meditation doesn't have to be more complicated than finding a quiet spot, getting comfortable, closing your eyes and breathing. Try the 7/11: slowly extend your breath until you're breathing in for a count of 7 and out for a count of 11. Instant, easy calm.

Learn from the experts

Find out whether your local Buddhist centre offers beginner sessions and go along to one. Or consider signing up to a course in Vedic meditation.

Join an Instagram Live

Keep your eye out for free live meditations on the gram. Lots of meditation teachers and mystical influencers offer regular sessions like this that anyone can join.

Choose a guide

Many well-known spiritual authors and speakers offer free meditation downloads online if you sign up to their mailing list. I really like *Rise Sister Rise* author Rebecca Campbell's Inner Temple meditation (rebeccacampbell.me).

Try a sound bath

If you find meditation tricky, sound can be the perfect way to relax and switch off. See the 'Soothe your soul with sound' section of the February chapter for ideas.

Set a timer

You don't even have to start at five minutes. Try three and see how it goes.

Perfect your shavasana

If you already practise yoga you can learn a lot about the benefits of meditation in *shavasana*. All of yoga is meditative in a way, but those few minutes at the end where you lie still could easily become the start of a regular meditation practice.

June

PLAY YOUR CARDS RIGHT

Celebration: Litha (summer solstice)

Moon: Strawberry moon

Sign: Gemini

Crystal: Agate

Element: Air

Tarot: The Lovers

Tarot tales

'You've always had the power, my dear,
you just had to learn it for yourself.'

GLINDA, THE GOOD WITCH OF THE NORTH, *THE WIZARD OF OZ*

I'm 14 years old, it's Christmas Day, and I've sneaked off to my bedroom in the attic. I'm holding a parcel wrapped in thin gold paper – a gift from my friends, my teenage coven. The best saved till last. The house smells of clementines and wood smoke. My bedroom smells of incense.

I press play on a mix tape and Massive Attack fades into Saint Etienne. I rip off the paper, knowing that inside I'll find the Christmas present I wanted most of all: my first tarot deck. The 1JJ Swiss, with French titles and woodcut images in bold primary colours. I shuffle. I lay out the cards. And it's as if a light turns on.

I'm 16 and lying flat on my back surrounded by springy purple heather. My friends and I survey our kingdom from the top of Yorkshire's Ilkley Moor. Big-sky views, wild expanses, magic in the air. We watch stars shoot across the summer night sky and trace our fingers over ancient stone carvings. We talk to wandering strangers about the meaning of life.

And when everything goes quiet and the moon shines bright, we slip through the broken boards of a derelict mansion to light candles and pull cards and join fingers over a homemade Ouija board.

I'm 18 and leaving Yorkshire for university in Liverpool. The cards are the first thing I pack. My eyes are ringed in two-day-old eyeliner and I'm trying hard not to cry it off. I've broken my first boyfriend's heart in my quest to be free. I've said dramatic farewells to friends I'll actually see again at Christmas. I'm high on histrionics and the magical misery of a life that's ending and beginning all at the same time.

I'm 23 and my parents have split up. My foundations have crumbled. The rug is no longer under me. My dad tells me that 'it's all part of life's rich tapestry', but my mum calls me crying at dawn.

I'm trying to become someone. I've just started a new job. I'm meant to be an adult now. But things are not okay. There's a weight on my chest and a lump in my throat. And I sink and I sink and there's no escape. It's as if I'm watching my life from above now. I scatter the tarot cards around my feet and see what lands face up.

I'm 29 and on the edge of something. I have decisions to make. And places to be. I have drinks waiting for me at a hot new bar that's just opened in London's Shoreditch. I've turned going out into a career and the party never stops. I can't take the heat but the kitchen is serving margaritas and I've a review to file by Monday morning. I know there's more to life than this but I don't know what that might be. Is this beautiful? Am I damned? Is it written in the stars? I spread the cards and look for the answers that are meant to be within me. Marriage and a mortgage and children and life. I pull the Two of Cups. And when he asks, I say yes.

Somehow, I'm 40. Growing up was a trick. I'm burnt out. I'm exhausted. I'm in the basement trying to remember what the hell I came down here for. Life feels like one big complicated question to which I'll never know the answer. I look in the box and I find the cards.

There may have been a hiatus where they gathered dust among the basement junk, but that 90s tarot deck has played a seriously important role in my life. Right down to kick-starting my whole mystical year. Good job, too. Because even when you're busy doing yoga and chanting mantras and asking the universe for signs, life still has a habit of throwing up way more questions than it ever gets round to answering.

I mean, what does a girl have to do to get a little help around here? Turn to the tarot, that's what.

If your mind has just skipped straight to stereotypical visions of spooky séances or fortune-tellers brandishing Death cards, I get it. There are a lot of misconceptions about tarot. Some people are downright terrified of it. But I've never seen the cards predict doom, gloom and certain death while cupboards open and close independently. Not so far, anyway. Tarot, for me, is simply a useful guidance tool that makes tapping in to our intuition (or inner knowing) a much easier task.

A spread of tarot cards is like a series of signposts waiting to be interpreted by the reader.

Interpretations that – quite rightly – could see the same cards in the same positions tell a completely different story from one day to the next. And that ominous-looking skeleton of Death? It usually signals the end of a cycle or even a shiny new beginning, rather than the moment you'll meet your maker.

Tarot is a tool I've turned to many times in my life. I've used tarot to navigate heartbreak, brave career changes and seek reassurance when the shit has hit the fan. I've read cards for friends desperate to know if the object of their desire will ever love them back or if they should quit their job to chase a dream. I've pulled cards at dinner parties, by office water coolers and on the top deck of the night bus home.

I've used the cards to ask myself difficult questions. And I've seen them call people out on issues that have been holding them back for years. I totally believe in the power of proper long-term therapy, but I've never known anything cut to the chase quite like tarot. You might want to cling on to the hope that your cheating ex can change, and your friends might skirt around the issue, saying what they think you want to hear, but tarot will serve up The Tower (which represents change, upheaval and endings) so fast you won't know what's hit you.

As my mystical year approached the halfway mark, I was finding the cards more insightful than ever. I bought a beautiful new deck called *The Starchild Tarot* and began pulling a card on mornings when I felt that a bit of extra guidance was needed (Six of Wands – success, progress – don't mind if I do!)

I found myself sitting cross-legged on my bed taking notes on elaborate card spreads again – just as I'd done all those years ago. I also began picking out inspiring cards to place on the makeshift altar of magical manifestation items I'd created in a corner of my bedroom.

Insights, guidance, inspiration… if there's an easier fast track to magic than tarot, I really don't know what it is. Tarot is a process, a to and fro. A conversation between the part of you that thinks it knows what's going on and the secret, hidden parts that actually do. It's not about predicting the future or definitive statements on how your life is going to turn out. It's about *feeling* your own way to the answer. Tuning in. Getting real. And, often, totally calling yourself out.

To me, tarot is a gift. And what I don't mean by that is that I have a special gift for reading the cards. I mean that they're a gift, end of. I believe that anyone can read tarot. The idea that you need to seek out a reading from someone with special psychic powers makes no sense to me at all.

That doesn't mean there's no value in paying for a reading; I love having my cards read by other people and it can be hugely insightful to hear someone else's interpretation of a spread. But honestly, the best readings I've ever had were DIY. Which comes in handy when my awkward call-outs from the universe are ones I'd prefer to absorb in private!

Do it yourself – tune in to tarot

To read tarot all you need to do is get your hands on a deck and find the time and inclination to start your own journey with the cards. Which brings us neatly onto another common misconception: that your first deck must always be received as a gift. I mean, you could be waiting a long time here. This is what self-gifting was invented for.

If you want in but don't already own a tarot deck (or you don't feel connected to the deck you do have), get out there and buy yourself one with imagery that speaks to you. There are many beautiful modern tarot decks to pick from (see the June entry in the Spiritual

Sourcebook for my recommendations), but don't be afraid to start with an old-style traditional deck if it feels right for you (the imagery on these can sometimes be easier for beginners to interpret).

It's important to note here that the tarot decks we think of as old-style or traditional (the 1JJ Swiss or Rider-Waite tarot deck, for example) are in fact later versions of cards that originated hundreds of years ago. The origins of tarot go back to Renaissance France and Italy, where decks evolved as high-society card games and, later, divination tools.

Earlier decks had some variation in the number of cards but bag yourself one today, and you'll generally find a standard 78 cards. Of that magic 78, 22 cards form the *Major Arcana* (all the big hitters you hope will show up in a spread – The Lovers, The Sun, The Star – and the intimidating ones you're not so sure about, like Death and The Tower) and 56 form the *Minor Arcana*, which is divided into four suits (see below), much like a standard pack of cards.

Individual decks differ slightly in imagery and terminology but the Major Arcana usually begins with The Fool and ends with The World, taking us on a journey through life, while the Minor Arcana represents the four elements (earth, air, fire, water), each of which depicts a different side of life within a numerological journey from Ace to King.

The Major Arcana cards indicate bigger life changes, lessons, or overarching themes while the Minor Arcana take a more close-up view, dealing with day-to-day life in all its glory. Don't despair if this is a lot to take in – the only real way to learn tarot is to get shuffling, and once you do that, it'll soon make sense.

To read tarot, you shuffle the cards while ruminating on a life situation or challenge and then pull one for guidance or a selection for a 'spread' (a layout of cards where each position relates to an area of life, a lesson, or a question to be answered). Then you start interpreting. Spreads can be as simple as three cards (representing past, present and future influences) or more in-depth readings where the meanings for each card encompass things like your strengths, weaknesses and outside influences.

I love a Celtic Cross spread (a traditional 10-card spread) but there are endless combinations and ideas out there (most Instagram tarot accounts create spreads you can use for DIY readings). You can even design your own spread to generate the exact guidance you need right now – anything goes!

This might all seem a bit complicated (which is why there's a handy Tarot 101 below to help you get your head around it), but the good news is that you don't need to memorize anything to read your own cards if you don't want to.

Firstly, you can look up the card meanings in the guidebook that accompanies your deck, and secondly, tarot can also be read completely intuitively. It really can be as easy as making some time, shuffling your deck, laying out a spread and just looking at the images on the cards and asking yourself what they're here to tell you. The more you do it, the more you'll realize you're getting it right. Every single time.

Because no one knows you like the inner you. Because your intuition is your superpower. Because with tarot as your guide, the future is yours.

Tarot 101

As you'll see in the guidebook that accompanies your deck there's a lot more to each card's meaning than those I've given below (including the fact the cards have alternate meanings when they appear reversed) – so consider this a quick reference guide to the main themes of a card when it appears upright in a reading.

I've used traditional card names and meanings; note that the Rider-Waite tarot deck swaps the positions of the Strength and Justice cards and more modern decks may use different imagery and names for some cards.

The Major Arcana

The Fool 0 – Beginnings, inexperience, a leap into the unknown

The Magician I – Creation, originality, potential, manifestation, ideas and action

The High Priestess II – Intuition, answers within, the subconscious

The Empress III – Feminine power, motherhood, beauty, achievement, nature, abundance

The Emperor IV – Authority, control, structure, power, fatherhood or father figures, wealth, stability

The Hierophant V – Wisdom, spirituality, morals, conformity, tradition, forgiveness, humility

The Lovers VI – Love, harmony, desire, close relationships

The Chariot VII – Forward motion, success, determination, overcoming the odds, steps towards a goal

Justice VIII – Truth, fairness, moderation, karma

The Hermit IX – Introspection, inner guidance, solitude, self-denial

Wheel of Fortune X – Luck, fate, destiny, progress, a change or turning point

Strength XI – Inner strength, courage, compassion, bravery

The Hanged Man XII – Limbo, pause, sacrifice, surrender, letting go, a change of mind

Death XIII – Endings, change, beginnings, transformation

Temperance XIV – Finding balance, calm, moderation, purpose

The Devil XV – Shadows, secrets, seduction, addiction, playing with fire, feeling trapped

The Tower XVI – Change, chaos, crumbling, sudden realizations

The Star XVII – Hope, inspiration, renewal, healing, purpose

The Moon XVIII – Illusions, misunderstandings, deception, intuition, feelings, fears

The Sun XIX – Fun, freedom, success, positivity, rewards, good vibes all round

Judgement XX – A calling, a higher good, decisions under review, rebirth

The World XXI – Completion, satisfaction, accomplishment, success, recognition or acclaim

The Minor Arcana

The 56 cards of the Minor Arcana are divided into four suits, each of which represents a different element and area of influence.

Wands (fire) – Energy, ambition, creativity, motivation, passion

Cups (water) – Emotions, relationships, feelings, spirituality, intuition, love

Swords (air) – Ideas, logic, thoughts, action, change

Coins/Pentacles or Crystals in some modern decks (earth) –
Career, finances, possessions, health, stability

Numerology of the Minor Arcana

Each suit is made up of 10 numbered cards and four Court cards
(Page, Knight, Queen and King; these often represent people in
your life in a reading). Each card has a unique meaning but as
a general guide, the numerology of tarot is a starting point for
getting to grips with your deck.

Ace – Beginnings

2 – Balance, choices, duos

3 – Groups, expression, creative growth

4 – Structure, foundations, manifestation

5 – Conflict, change, imbalances

6 – Harmony, good vibes, communication

7 – Reflection, knowledge, wisdom

8 – Action, achievement, effort

9 – Success, rewards, fulfilment

10 – Completion, transition, end of a cycle

Page – Youth, innocence, learning, inspiration

Knight – Travel, movement, idealism, future thinking

Queen – Nurturing, caring, feminine power

King – Power, authority, control, protection

You are the oracle

'I'm not The Goblin.'

ME

'Mama, I dropped my fork!'

'But I wanted the pink one!'

'You know I don't like that ketchup anymore!'

'Mummy, she's shouting at me!'

'She elbowed me!'

'Mama, I dropped my fish finger!'

'Mummy… Mum… Mama…'

'What's for pudding, Mama?'

'Can you not see I'm trying to activate an oracle deck on the internet, sweeties? Hold on a minute!'

As far as divination cards are concerned, tarot has always been my bag, so why I was attempting to combine the chaos of kids' teatime with a live online oracle card activation by spiritual author and deck creator Rebecca Campbell was anyone's guess. But there I was all the same: baby wipes in one hand, a selection of ketchup alternatives in the other, trying to simultaneously listen to Campbell and deck artist Danielle Noel talk on Zoom about the inspiration behind their new oracle deck, *Work Your Light*.

Although I was a long-time trawler of bookshop occult sections and patchouli-scented mystical emporiums, I'd never caught the oracle card bug. I'd bypassed them as birthday gifts, ignored them online and, after one particularly awkward yoga class in late 00s Bristol, I'd sworn off them completely when at the end of the session the teacher invited us all to pull a card from a fairy deck and I got The Goblin.

Yep, The Goblin.

I remember staring at it as we waited for her to read out, one by one, the meanings of the cards we'd chosen. Uplifting words about fairy queens and magical elves and new beginnings and untold joy. I turned my card over so The Goblin would stop staring at me. I was last in the circle so I knew I was the only person with a 'bad' card.

'Erm, so I got The Goblin,' I said, as 10 pairs of eyes turned to bore into my soul. The teacher started to read about my wounded ego and sped up as she got to the chaos this was undoubtedly causing in my life. The eyes politely looked away. It was just a card, but I felt judged. 'I'm not The Goblin,' I whispered. But somehow I knew that I was.

I was pretty confident that the *Work Your Light* oracle deck sitting on my crumb-covered kitchen counter was going to be a Goblin-free zone. It was also my first ever set of oracle cards. I knew I had to have them the second they appeared on my radar because Danielle Noel (creator of my adored *The Starchild Tarot* deck) was the artist behind the illustrations. I've never thought of myself as the dreamily ethereal type but there's something about her art that just speaks to me. Let me step into that soft-focus pastel world and commune with those magical beings, already. I knew I'd love these cards from the off.

There was something familiar about Rebecca Campbell, too. I'd recently started reading her book *Rise Sister Rise* and her earlier title *Light is the New Black* was ready to go on my tower of mystical bedtime reading.

But that wasn't it. I'd seen her somewhere before. It took me a while to remember that it had been on my friend Leesa's Facebook feed two years earlier. Leesa had uploaded a video of Rebecca speaking ahead of a one-day *Rise Sister Rise* workshop, and I was pretty sure I could remember scrolling past it, thinking I'd never be able to find the time to attend something like that.

But here I was now, with Rebecca Campbell on the screen in front of me, fully engaged – well, as fully engaged as a person whose daughter has just spilt orange juice all over the kitchen can be. The further my mystical year progressed, the more I appreciated such synchronicities and I found myself noticing signposts that had been there all along.

It was strangely affirming to think that the path that had led me to this particular oracle deck might have been laid some years ago. I liked the idea that things might appear in my field of vision for a reason. And that even if I'd dismissed them the first time around, they'd probably try me again. Could it be that I was being nudged by the universe, even back then in 2016? I really liked that thought. I also liked the thought of escaping the fish finger chaos and hiding upstairs in my bedroom.

'Chocolate for pudding, if you let me watch this for the next 30 minutes, girls.'

It was game on. I couldn't wait to get stuck into this particular mystical adventure. In fact, I couldn't believe it had taken me so long to get on board with oracle cards.

> ✦ *Tarot's easy, breezy, little sister – you only have to flick through an oracle deck to know it's a more instantly accessible guidance tool.*

There are fewer cards, for starters (just 44 of them in *Work Your Light*), and there are no traditional meanings to get bogged down by. In fact, the meanings are often written on the cards themselves so you need never flick through the accompanying guidebook if you don't want to. And you definitely don't need to sign up to an expensive course that promises to reveal some magic secret to reading them, because there isn't one. I know I said that tarot is the most straightforward and easy way to add magic to your life, but oracle cards might just be even easier.

I'm not sure whether online activations or attunements, like the one I was trying not to be distracted from, are standard practice in the oracle deck world, but I wouldn't recommend attempting to join one while your children hammer on your bedroom door anyway. That said, my girls were happily covering themselves in chocolate now, so I was free to return to the video call.

The introductory chat was over and it was time to attune and activate. I put on my headphones and followed along. I breathed in. I breathed out. I attempted to locate my inner temple. I visualized a water lily slowly unfurling to reveal a universe of starry lights within me. I joined a collective incantation to the wisdom keepers of the Earth and held the cards above my head to connect with my soul star chakra.

I felt faintly ridiculous; however, as with so many of the mystical adventures I'd been on this year, I could see that this was mostly about creating space. By allowing myself even this small amount of time away from the maelstrom of domestic responsibility, I was somehow saying to the universe that I was ready to tune in, to use my intuition, and work out my purpose in life. And I reckoned these cards were going to help me do it.

Shame my daughters didn't get the memo! Someone's iPad was running out of battery. Someone's eye hurt. Someone wanted to know if she could have more chocolate because the ones I'd given her were 'really, really, very extremely tiny'. Good job I'd decided that the online attunement was an optional extra rather than a mystical essential. I shouted 'bathtime' down the stairs, took a deep breath and then pulled my first card from the deck.

Many mystics believe that the first card you pull from a new deck contains a particularly poignant or important message. I had about two seconds to spare but I was ready for mine: *MINTAKAN. Longing for home. Belonging. The original Lightworkers.*

The accompanying image was beautiful – a mermaid gazing out onto the dreamiest of water worlds – but I didn't have a clue what it meant. I'd picked this deck for its magical imagery without much thought about what was behind the *Work Your Light* title or what the cards' meanings might be. Turned out I might need to look up a few things in the accompanying guidebook after all!

What I found there needed rather more attention than my two-kids-and-a-running-bath set-up was able to provide, but I was instantly intrigued. The explanation suggested I might belong to a soul group that originated on a planet in the constellation Orion.

I was a star being, a Starseed – a soul that first incarnated somewhere way beyond planet Earth!

How about that for a random Tuesday evening revelation? I wasn't quite sure if I was feeling it, but I definitely wanted to know more. I sat on the edge of the bath, clutching my phone in a Googling frenzy.

It's said that people who identify as Starseeds often feel as if they don't fit in. They might also feel homesick for a place that they can't quite describe, or feel strongly connected to a certain type of landscape yet be unable to explain why. All pretty relatable, if you ask me. It's also believed that Starseeds have a mission of good to complete here on Earth, which is presumably where the 'original Lightworkers' thing comes in.

I'd often seen the word Lightworker bandied about on inspirational Instagram posts since my mystical year began but I hadn't given a huge amount of thought to what it meant. I think I'd assumed it referred to some kind of magical energy healing or psychic ability or communication with angels – something otherworldly and mysterious that I'd probably never understand. It turned out to be far more straightforward.

A Lightworker is anyone who's working to make the world a better place. It's also someone who believes they are part of a bigger collective force for good; someone who shares their light in large or small ways, follows their truth, and believes in a better world for everyone. I couldn't argue with that. So why was my head still in a spin about my first-pull Mintakan card?

I suppose it all just seemed a bit out-there. Was this really a thing? Did I really once live in a world with water so pure and clear you could see through it for miles? Was I really one of the original Lightworkers? This was the kind of new identity I could imagine getting on board with, but not without some serious adjustment time!

I put the card back in the deck and turned my attention to children and iPad chargers and clothes scattered over bedroom floors, my mind whirring. I *have* always had a major thing for water, I thought. Come to think of it, I've always had a bit of a thing for Orion (as a child, his belt was the second constellation I learnt to spot in the night sky). Was there something in this? Do souls really incarnate on faraway stars?

I Googled Mintaka – it really was a star in Orion's belt. It all sounded wonderfully magical. I loved the idea of collective good and changing the world for the better. And it was definitely the best excuse I'd heard for not quite feeling the whole life-on-planet-Earth thing. Yet it also felt like a very big rabbit hole to fall down on a school night; and the bath was about to overflow.

I picked up the cards and shuffled them again, holding them out to my daughters, Lola and Cleo. We each picked one: 'Dance' and 'Play' and 'Take a Break'. Ah, that was better. That I *could* roll with, no Googling required. So that's what we did. Taylor Swift on the speaker, bubbles in the bath, phone stashed away out of sight and out of mind. Bathroom mirror peace signs, fluffy white bubble beards, flush-cheeked laughter wrapped up in warm towels. And, of course, all the unicorn chat.

I doubt my girls would struggle to believe that their mother is a being from a magical planet. They believe in everything. My new deck may have thrown me a curveball that I didn't quite know what to do with, but it followed it up with *exactly* what I needed to get through another night on the domestic front line.

And a week later another one-card pull gave me the straightest answer to a question I'd ever got from a deck of cards. My editor had emailed to ask if I could write the feature I'd suggested weeks earlier for the magazine's September issue. She knew I'd stopped working on the website and she knew my invoices were still unpaid. She was in the same situation herself but had decided to press on regardless.

I knew that writing the feature would help her out, and every bone in my people-pleasing body wanted to say yes and fix it. But my instincts told me it just wasn't right. I decided to turn to the *Work Your Light* oracle deck for a bit of extra guidance. I shuffled all 44 cards, spread them out in front of me and picked just one: it was the 'No' card. It couldn't have been clearer, and it was the confirmation I needed to respond once again in a way that I couldn't have imagined myself doing a year earlier: 'I'm sorry, I can't. No.'

I'm not saying that I wouldn't have reached that conclusion anyway, but I reached it sooner with that deck in hand. And therein lies the magic of oracle cards. They're easy. They're accessible. And you're in charge. They might call you out. They might show you something you know you needed to hear. You can take a message and run with it or put it on the back burner for a less complicated time (hello, magical Mintakan water world!) It's pocket guidance that, more often than not, hits exactly the right spot. As mystical fixes go, I reckon it's a straight-up win.

Do it yourself – become the oracle

If you're intrigued enough to want in with oracle cards, all you need to do is choose a deck of cards you like the look of, connect to them, shuffle them, and most importantly, use them.

Each morning, pull one card and let its meaning guide your day. Read a spread for yourself at the start of each month. Pick three cards (past, present and future) on the new moon or the full moon or any time you like. Take the guidance and run with it. As often as feels right to you.

It shouldn't be difficult to find your perfect oracle cards. There are decks out there to suit all interests and mystical persuasions – open the floodgates and you might find that you want them all. There are animal decks and angel decks and goddess decks and moon decks. There are accompanying guidebooks full of beautifully thought-out meanings that make goose bumps feel like a permanent affliction and magical illustrations you wish you could step right into.

If you love cats, choose a cat deck. If you want to get called out by a goblin, choose a fairy deck. If you fancy a brand new planet to call home, the beautiful *Work Your Light* oracle cards definitely have you covered. There's an oracle with your name on it and it's out there waiting for you.

The inscription inside the *Work Your Light* deck box sums it up for me: 'You are the oracle.' And you know what? I think I am. And, even if you don't quite know it yet, you are too.

Three card spreads

These simple spreads can be used for both oracle and tarot card readings.

Past, present, future spread

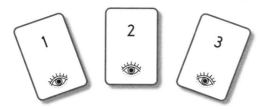

1. Past influences that are having an impact on your life right now

2. What you need now, in your present situation

3. What lies ahead in the near future for you

Relationship spread

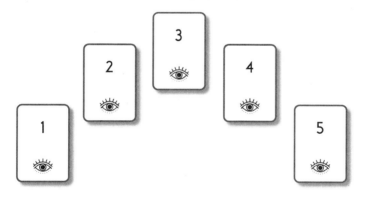

1. You right now

2. Your partner right now

3. What your relationship is built on

4. Current issues affecting your relationship

5. Where all this is going to end up

New Year spread

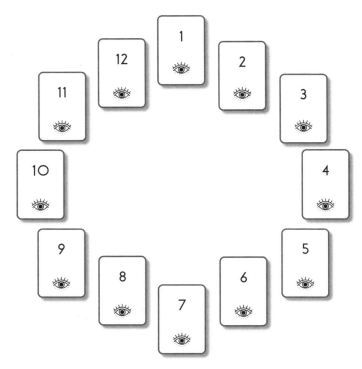

1. What lies ahead in January

2. Your vibe for February

3. What's happening in March

4. April magic

5. How May looks for you

6. A magical June

7. Get set for July

8. Watch out for this in August

9. September changes

10. Good times in October

11. What awaits you in November

12. How you'll end the year

Six Months In

Fiona
Emma's been quiet on WhatsApp recently. Anyone heard from her?
9:34

Katherine
Some crazy stuff about the magazine going under, but I don't think it's official yet. The cards told her not to write for them anymore!
9:36

Sarah
😂 🙄
Emma! Emma! Are you out there?
9:37

Emma
Yep! Here! And it's all true! Unfortunately!
10:15✓✓

Bethan
So, have you found yourself yet?
10:20

Emma
Not sure, but I have discovered that my soul may have incarnated in the constellation Orion many light years ago...
10:22✓✓

Bethan
That explains a lot!
10:23

Emma
And it looks like I've got the summer off work!
10:25✓✓

Katherine
Every mystical cloud...
10:26

July

GARDEN SHED HEALERS & CRYSTAL MYTHS

Celebration: St Swithin's Day

Moon: Buck moon

Sign: Cancer

Crystal: Moonstone

Element: Water

Tarot: The Chariot

The ego has landed

'The wound is the place where
the Light enters you.'
RUMI

'Can anyone recommend an amazing local reiki practitioner?'

I'd spent six whole months trying to make my life better with yoga, meditation and midnight pleas to the moon – it was high time I called in a professional.

I waited for Facebook to respond... Names. More names. Links. Recommendations. A couple of 'DM me's'. A trio of eye-roll emojis. And one 'This is simultaneously the most ridiculous AND middle-class recommendation request I have ever seen!' Middle class? I wondered if it was because I'd specified a need for local sourcing.

I laughed to myself (and at myself) and immediately began Googling the list of options my request had generated. There's nothing quite like the sense of panic induced by looming school summer holidays to get a mystical thinker to up her game. If I was going to make it through the end-of-term shows and emails and lost PE sock WhatsApp messages with my inner peace intact, this was not the time to lose momentum.

Before long, I'd found a reiki practitioner with a slew of gushing recommendations. I didn't know that much about healers or healing therapies, but I did know a bit about reiki. And it's a treatment that (usually) involves lying down for an hour and a half – what's not to like?

✧ *Reiki is a Japanese alternative therapy based around the concept of channelling universal energy to promote healing and relaxation.*

Dr Mikao Usui developed his reiki system in the 1920s but it wasn't until the 1980s and 90s that the hands-on (or off – reiki can also be practised at a distance) therapy became more commonplace in the Western wellness world.

I'd tried reiki once before, many years earlier. My best friend Katherine's sister was one of its early adopters; a respected reiki master who went on to become one of the first practitioners to introduce energy healing as a complementary therapy within the NHS, Claudia was freshly trained and looking for people to practise on as the new millennium dawned.

It just so happened that around that time I was falling apart. My world had gone black. My parents were getting divorced and I felt as if the foundation on which I'd set out to build my life had crumbled to dust. I'd moved to London to chase a dream that felt like it might be too aspirational for someone like me. I wanted to be a writer but I didn't come from the kind of family that had emergency funds or trust funds or the spoils of self-made success earning interest in a bank account somewhere. I couldn't afford to do the months of unpaid work experience that appeared to be the only route into the glossy magazine world I wanted to inhabit. I needed to work – for actual money!

I'd won a place on a prestigious postgraduate journalism course, but the thought of building up a big debt while I did it led me to decline the opportunity. The one thing I'd always known I could fall back on – my neat little parental double act (and I realize that having had that at all was a privilege) – had somehow spiralled into something more complicated.

I hadn't realized how much of a security blanket that 'forever roof over my head' back home in Yorkshire had been, until the day I withdrew rent money on a credit card while my mum emptied the marital home into a skip. 'Just chuck away anything of mine,' I told her. 'I'm so sorry I'm not there helping.'

It felt as if the tide was against me, but it was also sink or swim time. Katherine – my light in all storms since the freezing cold November day she befriended me at university – decided I was going to swim, and that her newly trained healer sister would be the one to help me do it.

I don't remember much about the reiki treatment itself, other than how glad I was that no clothing had to be removed and how novel it was to lie down with my eyes closed and not go to sleep. What I do recall very clearly is Claudia's voice gently telling me things that seemed obvious and revelatory at the same time: look after yourself, drink more water, if you hold your stomach in all the time you can't breathe properly.

I remember thinking it all sounded so simple, and wondering why I'd never thought about looking after myself before. Or drinking water. Or breathing out. I definitely remember leaving her treatment room feeling extremely relaxed and peaceful. I hadn't quite ditched the miserable feeling that I was watching my own fractured life from above, but whatever she'd done in there had made it feel more like a protective bubble. I felt impenetrable, as though nothing else could hurt me.

That reiki session definitely helped pull me out of a slump. It buoyed me up enough to send myself to therapy and start taking back control. And now, nearly two decades later and as a fully fledged mystical thinker, my hope was that a spot of reiki would wave the right kind of magic wand over the rest of 2018.

I got my friend Laura on board for another mystical adventure and contacted the recommended practitioner to see if I could book a couple of back-to-back sessions. And after a Facebook DM exchange that referenced talking to horses and the vagina of life, I knew I'd found my woman!

On a stifling hot day, Laura and I pulled up outside a cottage in Kent to be greeted by Myra, a gravelly voiced blonde who was as straight talking in real life as she'd been in her DMs. It was vaguely unnerving. I'd become conditioned to expect mystical types to be ethereal and softly spoken, and yet here was this confident, bold presence in jeans and a fringed jacket.

Myra seemed more like someone I'd have a laugh with over a few drinks than the mystical answer to all my problems, and I also couldn't quite shake the feeling that she could see right through me. From the start of our amusing Facebook exchange, I'd had a hunch that this would be no ordinary reiki treatment.

I was ready. But Myra, it appeared, wasn't quite.

'You're both here,' she said, as if it was a question.

'Erm, yes!' I replied.

'At the same time, I mean. I wasn't expecting that,' Myra continued.

I suddenly felt bad about the double person invasion: 'Oh, sorry. We thought it made sense to drive over together. Maybe one of us can wait in the car?'

'No, it's okay! One of you can sit in the garden while I do the other,' Myra said, gesturing towards an ornament-strewn patio.

'I'll go first,' I whispered to Laura. 'Then I can write up some notes while you have your treatment.'

I'm not sure what kind of treatment room I thought I'd find at this cottage in the middle of nowhere, but I realized that I'd been spoilt by swanky hotel sound baths and sleek yoga studios with woodland views when Myra pointed the way to a garden shed. A *shed*! Was I seriously about to try and get my zen on in a shed?

I quickly corrected myself. What the hell had I expected – a luxury treatment room in some distant mansion wing with complimentary cucumber water? No, of course not. I was not that person. I was fine with a shed.

A damned good shed it was too. There was fabric pinned across the ceiling, fairy lights twinkling from wall to wall and crystals dotted on every spare surface. Myra was chatting away about what to expect from the session when it hit me: I could feel the energy of this place already. It felt like something major was about to go down. I got up on the treatment table and closed my eyes.

There was distant music. There were incantations. This wasn't the silent, hands-on reiki treatment I'd had all those years earlier with Claudia. This felt like something else entirely. Myra's voice was low and mesmerizing as she talked me through my chakras – from the golden-brown earth star chakra below my feet to the soul star chakra above my head – describing a whole starry universe in the process.

I'd never really tried to connect to my chakras – the energy centres of the body – before, but I could see them all clearly in my mind's eye now: a rainbow of light from root to crown. Myra seemed to be speaking a language I didn't understand but which somehow made sense to me all the same. I felt her hands both hot and cold on different parts of my body.

Sometimes it felt as if there was more than one of her. As if there was a whole cosmic team working together to create something that was so much more than just relaxation and way less calming than healing. It was more like an awakening or a rebirth (quite possibly through life's vagina?). At times, she talked me through what she was doing – cutting cords, shifting blockages, allowing energy to flow – at others she was silent bar the occasional click of the tongue.

I didn't know quite what this was, or if it was legit, or whether a reiki governing body would approve of her methods, but I was totally into it. My mind was firing on all cylinders. I could see colours and faces and shapes, and somehow I could hear and feel them too. I saw stars burst into tiny fragments before me. I saw a snake rise up from the Earth. Did I mention I have an impressive imagination?

I felt as if I could really see for the first time that everything in the universe is connected.

But there was a panicky, urgent feeling too. It felt like a truth was about to be revealed to me. It was so close I could almost touch it and yet it was just out of reach. Before I could find it, the treatment was over.

I felt as if I was on another planet. This wasn't the dreamy, relaxed feeling I'd experienced with sound baths or yoga. It was different. I asked Myra if she thought she'd learnt anything about me from

A YEAR OF MYSTICAL THINKING

doing the treatment. She got it in one when she told me that I was all in my head and totally ungrounded. I'd never felt less grounded in my life. It felt as if I was on fire. But in a good way – as if I was burning with the kind of energy that never runs out.

That's when the realization hit me – and it was one that I felt instantly compelled to voice. I'm not normally the free and easy sharing type so hearing my inner monologue spoken out loud was pretty unnerving: 'I just don't fit in here, in this part of the world,' I said. 'It all feels too showy, too materialistic. Too busy. Too exhausting. It's not for me, but...'

'I hear you,' Myra interrupted. Was she trying to stop me from saying what I was going to say next?

'But...' I continued. 'I think that might be exactly why I ended up here. So I can show people that there's another way. That life doesn't have to be such a hustle. That it can all be so much easier. That there's magic in the world if you just take the time to look for it.'

Myra looked at me for what felt like a long time. I was sure she was about to nod sagely and confirm that everything I'd said was true. I felt as though she had the power to affirm me and send me on my way, out into the world to wave a magic wand over everything I found difficult or painful or sad. I looked back at her, my feet swinging as I sat on the edge of the bed.

'That's just your ego talking,' she said eventually, as she folded a sarong. 'That's all just ego.'

I felt crushed, and I didn't know how to react. I was so sure I'd hit on the answer to everything! Why wasn't she telling me what I wanted to hear?

'Trying to change those outside yourself is a very difficult path to take,' Myra added.

I opened my mouth to speak but nothing came out. I didn't know whether to laugh or cry. But it was Laura's turn in the magic shed so I slipped out and sat with my notebook in the sunshine, contemplating my own stupid ego.

Had it really been my ego talking? I felt like I barely *had* an ego. I'd spent my whole life being what other people wanted me to be. Liking people because they liked me. Choosing people because they chose me. Being good. Being kind. Trying to fit in. I wasn't even sure I had a very strong concept of self. Was I really someone who had an ego that needed keeping in line?

If you look up the *Collins English Dictionary*'s definition of the word ego, being told you have one that's 'doing the talking' doesn't exactly feel flattering: 'Someone's ego is their sense of their own worth. For example, if someone has a large ego, they think they are very important and valuable.'

I don't know about you, but thinking of myself as very important and valuable feels totally alien. And I can't think of anything I'd like less than being described as big-headed. Most of us are simply not brought up that way, right? Modest, humble, self-deprecating – I pretty much live by that code.

But is having an ego really such a bad thing? Most people I know could do with upping their self-worth and self-belief a few notches. It didn't quite make sense to me that it was horribly egotistical to think I might have something to share with the world.

I'd studied psychology as part of my degree so I knew there was more depth to the concept of ego than just that awkward definition. I thought back to all those essays on Freud. In his model of the psyche the ego is the buffer zone that exists between the id (our subconscious pleasure-seeking animal instinct) and the super-ego (the moral compass and social conditioning that tells us what we 'should' be and feels guilt when we fail to live up to it). In this model, the ego is the good guy – the rational, realistic, sensible self that's mediating the other two! What's so bad about that?

I wasn't totally sure that either of those definitions were what Myra was getting at, though. There's a lot of talk about ego death in spiritual circles – the idea that in order to achieve enlightenment and true inner peace one needs to let the rational mind and self die completely. I wondered if this was more what she'd meant.

I also wondered if I should just go back and ask her, although I wasn't totally sure this was a can of worms I was ready to open. Maybe I did need to let my ego die. If I did, perhaps everything else would fall into place and I'd find nirvana. It'd certainly be nice to stop thinking so much for a while. I decided to stop writing notes and Googling ego death and soak up the sun with a book while I waited for Laura.

I was a few chapters into Gabrielle Bernstein's *Judgement Detox* and it had really got me thinking. Until I'd started reading it, I hadn't realized how judgemental I was. I was halfway through an exercise in which she asks the reader to witness their own judgement *without* judgement, which is much harder than it sounds! It was blowing my mind.

Basically, on a piece of paper, you create four columns and head each one with a question: 1. What or who am I judging? 2. How does this judgement make me feel? 3. Why do I feel justified in this judgement? 4. What moment in my life triggered me to feel justified in this judgement? And then you write down your response to the questions.

I'd come up with quite the list of responses, and it was such an eye-opener. I judged people for having political views that were different to mine, for thinking they're always right, for being showy about their wealth, for not reading to their children, for taking too many selfies, for spending so much on fast fashion, for joining multilevel marketing schemes that require them to flog dubious supplements to their mates, and for caring about cars and handbags and expensive kitchens.

I was a truly awful person! But the reasons behind my judgements were even more revealing. So often when I finally unearthed my triggers, it came down to thinking I wasn't good enough – and to some deep-rooted, unfulfilled need or desire I'd never really admitted to. I wasn't quite sure where I was going with all this self-analysis, but I did know that if I wanted to try and make a difference in the world, I'd probably have to stop judging it so harshly first. My session in the shed had shifted something.

I wanted to share and connect and make the world around me more beautiful somehow. It felt like a mission I wanted to accept.

Even if it *was* just my ego talking.

I waited for Laura to emerge and we made our escape. It turned out that her mind had been blown too.

'That was full on,' she said. 'I definitely need a glass of wine on the way home.'

'I think you might be right,' I replied.

We stopped at a country pub with a huge grassy garden and sipped as we soaked up the sunshine.

'I don't think I'll forget that in a hurry,' I remarked.

'She knew so many things about me, even though I gave nothing away,' said Laura.

'She made me feel as if I had a mission from the universe! And then a few minutes later, like I was the most insignificant person on Earth,' I said.

'Sounds awkward!' Laura replied.

'There was definitely something in it, though. It's got me thinking in a way I can't quite explain,' I said.

'It's made me wonder if that's what reiki's always like,' said Laura.

'Honestly,' I replied, 'I don't think it is. I think that was something else.'

Do it yourself – try energy healing

Energy healing has many different disciplines (reiki being one of the best known), all of which work on similar principles – channelling energy for relaxation and healing. There are also many energy-based therapies that work in similar ways, such as acupressure, qigong and reflexology. Below are some excellent reasons to give energy healing a try that are applicable to all disciplines.

Time out

How often do you take time out for yourself? Making room in your life for a treatment such as reiki (or any energy treatment) is a positive step towards a more balanced life.

Focus on you

Before a treatment most energy healing practitioners will take a bit of a medical/wellness history and talk you through ways you might be able to add more self-care to your life. If you don't often spend time focusing on yourself and your wellbeing, this can offer some valuable thinking time to consider these things.

Non-invasive

You don't have to remove any clothing or even lie down if that's uncomfortable for you (reiki can be done seated). Energy healing can take place in conjunction with conventional medical treatment (always check with your doctor first).

Relaxation

An hour-long energy healing treatment is an hour-long lie down with your eyes closed. Reduced stress, better emotional balance and a feeling of relaxation are the most commonly reported post-reiki session results.

Mind expanding

By allowing yourself time to truly relax you may find you're better able to tune in to your subconscious mind. This can be brilliant for creative thinking, problem solving or just working out what you really want out of life.

Connections

Energy healers tend to be an interesting bunch, whether they're careful followers of rules and regulations or slightly more maverick in their approach. If you're looking for connections or recommendations for other spiritual pursuits, a great energy healer can be a good starting point.

How to choose a healer

Start by asking friends, family and the internet for recommendations and then feel your way to the right person. Try to talk to them and ask what to expect from your first treatment, what they charge per session, and where they do their treatments. If you like the idea of a distant healing session you can cast your net as wide as you like since you won't have attend in person.

If you'd feel more comfortable with a practitioner who's registered with a regulatory body (see the July entry in the Spiritual Sourcebook) have a look at their listings. Local health and wellness stores and/or mind, body, soul events or festivals can also be great places to find recommendations for good practitioners.

Get stoned

'Crystals are the ultimate powerhouses of
the Earth. ready to raise your vibrations.'

EMMA LUCY KNOWLES

July was ticking by like a time bomb, and the countdown to the school holidays was now in single figures. I was determined to squeeze in another mystical adventure before I got sucked into the childcare void, and it felt like the perfect time to get to grips with crystals.

My Instagram feed was full of them. And every time I opened a magazine there was a gushing reference to the infinite magical powers of rose quartz or tourmaline. Naomi Campbell was into crystals. Adele was into crystals. Victoria Beckham was sewing secret stone pockets into her catwalk show trousers. Crystals were having one hell of a moment. And I was sure that if I was just a bit more tuned in to them, I'd be having one too.

I'd gathered quite a collection of small, shiny tumblestones since the start of the year and my magpie-like children had gathered even more. We'd even arranged our stash on the grass outside to charge under the full moon a couple of times. My girls were certain they could feel the extra magic of that moon power.

I knew that crystals were all about raising vibrations and tuning in, and that different stones had different properties, but it still wasn't quite clicking. The beautiful green moonstone sphere I'd bought in March had accompanied me on many a YouTube meditation session, but I didn't think it was really making a difference to my life.

It wasn't as if I'd never felt connected to a crystal before, either. I'd carried a rose quartz palm stone around with me throughout the second half of my pregnancy with my eldest daughter. It became a talisman that got me through bad news at the 20-week scan, a threatened premature labour at 29 weeks, a stressful emergency caesarean and some full-on postnatal anxiety. Fortunately, that's a story with a very happy ending and a pink stone stashed in a baby memory box next to a tiny pair of shoes.

And yet, despite that memory and the growing stash of stones in my house, the crystal craze seemed to be passing me by in 2018. It felt like a mental block. Healing stones, energetic vibrations, magical meanings: it all seemed so out-there. Was carnelian really going to make me braver? Could owning a piece of tiger's eye actually turn me into a creative genius? How did this all work?

There was another issue, too. Another online article – this time about crystal mining ethics – made me wonder if this was a spiritual pursuit destined for the think twice list. Stick yourself in front of a dreamy display of shiny coloured stones and it's easy to forget they were once part of the Earth itself. Of course, mining the Earth for profit is nothing new: I just couldn't fathom how it worked with the whole good vibes thing.

I looked for information on where the crystals I liked came from but it was difficult to find. I'm not sure whether some of the shop owners I asked even knew. In fact, the only shop I encountered that was able to provide information about its sourcing was SLC London. I bought myself two new stones from there (a large piece of raw rose quartz and a clear quartz point) and decided that was it for me until I could find a way to make sure other crystals I bought were equally traceable.

One good thing about this was that it made me more determined to connect to the stones I already had. If I'd caused them to be pulled from the Earth by buying them, surely the least I could do was try and make them work for me. And once I started tuning in, it didn't take long for the crystal magic to click into place.

There were two things that did it. First, I started reading Emma Lucy Knowles's book *The Power of Crystal Healing*. I'd been following her Instagram feed for a while and loved her modern approach to crystals and the good vibes she seemed to transmit through cyberspace. I liked her easy, chatty take on the subject. I'd always chosen crystals because I liked their colour or the idea of a healing property assigned to them, but she suggested choosing them intuitively instead. It felt like a game-changer.

To choose a crystal intuitively all you have to do is ignore your conscious mind (and all the things I mentioned above) and simply allow yourself to be drawn to the right one for you – and maybe cross your fingers that it doesn't turn out to be a £1,000 amethyst cave. The idea is that by letting instinct lead the way (with your eyes closed if you prefer), you end up with the right crystal, for the right purpose, at the right time.

Back then, anything that took decision making out of my hands was a winner, so I decided to put this process to the test using the crystals I already had. I laid out crystals large and small in an arc at one end of the kitchen table and spent a week picking the one I felt most drawn to that day before looking up its meaning in a book. It was an eye-opener.

One stressful Monday, when a broken printer, work deadlines and a four-page email from my children's school about end-of-term arrangements threatened to send my inner peace packing, I found myself drawn to a piece of pale blue lace agate. I looked it up and the meaning was spot on.

 Blue lace agate is a crystal thought to help with calming tired, stressed-out minds – exactly what I needed.

I stashed the stone in my jeans pocket, took a deep breath and chose to approach the day with a clear head and a decidedly lax approach to punctuality. It worked like a dream.

I had a date in my diary that week for end-of-term drinks on Thursday night; however, I had a big day at work planned for Friday and knew I couldn't risk any overenthusiasm on the rosé. I also knew that as soon as I had one glass in a sunny pub beer garden, I'd think another was a truly excellent idea. I closed my eyes and held my hands over the kitchen table stones until I got that 'feels right' feeling. I knew I'd nailed it the second I opened them. Amethyst: my birthstone.

I've long known the meaning of amethyst – a crystal thought to help with inner peace, psychic connection and controlling addictive behaviour. It's even known as the sobriety stone in some circles. I decided to take the hint. I put the stone in my bag and then sent an email to the end-of-term drinks group, offering to be designated driver. And I ignored all the protest that email caused. It was worth it: I've never felt quite so smugly efficient as I did that Friday morning.

The weekend was also set to be full on: a big school production at a local theatre followed by parties and celebrations and the sort of large groups of people my introverted heart always finds it tricky to deal with. I felt that I needed a protective stone – an inky black obsidian, perhaps, or a piece of smoky quartz – but my intuitive pick led me to citrine. Citrine is thought to be something of a powerhouse, a stone of abundance and optimism and good vibes galore.

Perhaps this was the call-out I needed. I tried swapping social anxiety for open-hearted optimism and threw myself into the sort of small talk I was used to finding painful. Before I knew it, with that yellowy stone stashed in my bag, I was having a genuinely brilliant time.

It was all starting to make sense to me but I wanted more. I found myself looking up crystal healers online and trying to work out how on earth I could fit in a session with my kids in tow. I was just about to write it off as impossible when a message appeared in my inbox from an Israeli jeweller called Odelia. She had a thing about crystals and wanted to offer me a crystal reading (a bit like a tarot reading but with stones) over Zoom. It felt as if the universe had intervened.

I packed the girls off to a friend's house and Odelia and I had a video call linking suburban Kent with Tel Aviv. I liked her instantly. And she totally had my number. We were about five minutes into the session when she called me out for typing up notes and only half listening to what she was saying.

'You need to focus on this,' she said. 'Record the call and don't think about how you're going to turn it into a blog post until later, okay?' I needed to be told.

I'd never had a crystal reading so I had no idea what was coming, but Odelia started with the kind of vocal intention setting to highest light and purpose I'd come to expect from my mystical endeavours.

She had a relaxed, chatty, lighthearted manner that made me feel instantly at ease – it was like talking with an old friend.

She explained that in person, we'd have all the crystals in front of us for me to hold and connect to, but that online I'd look at some images she'd prepared that would work just as well. Then she asked me a few questions about how things were for me at the moment, and it made me realize how rarely I talked about myself.

That might sound odd, given that this book is the story of a year of my life, but as a journalist my job has always been to tell other people's stories – to be the one asking the questions and tuning in to the truth behind the answers. As an introvert, my personal life tends to go the same way. My extrovert husband frequently despairs at my inability to communicate what I'm thinking and feeling. My friends always try and ply me with wine in the hope that I'll open up. Spilling the personal tea just doesn't come naturally to me, unless it's being channelled through my fingers onto a clean white page.

Still, Odelia was asking and it would be rude not to answer. So I told her how conflicted I was feeling about giving up my magazine job. And how even though I should probably be chasing freelance commissions, I'd found myself keeping my pitches to a minimum. I really wanted to spend some proper time with my children over the summer, instead of dealing with the usual have-it-all juggle. I also wanted to spend more time writing blog posts to share my mystical experiences.

The feeling I'd got in the reiki session with Myra hadn't left me. I still believed that I had a mission to connect other people to my favourite parts of the mystical world. But what if spending more time on all this stuff had a seriously negative impact on my earning power? What if, after my summer off, all the commissioning editors I knew stopped answering my emails? I was lucky to be married to someone with a sensible, regular job, so the family finances weren't about to flatline for the sake of a whim, but it still felt like a risk. A self-indulgent, poorly thought-out, potentially debt-inducing risk.

Odelia listened carefully and decided that my first question for the crystal reading should be: 'What will help me put my best foot forward into this new stage of my life?' Then she asked me to intuitively choose the crystal that was speaking to me most at that moment. I picked the one that always speaks to me most: amethyst. She said the first crystal in a reading normally reveals something you need to work on or a challenge. Then she told me what was coming through for her. That's when it all came out.

'Amethyst,' she said, 'is a stone of transformation and intuition. A stone that can help with addiction and purification. A stone that's great for meditating with.'

I soon found myself telling her that I was trying really hard not to get sucked into the wine o'clock culture that surrounded me. I admitted how uncomfortable I felt living among the shiny-haired wealth of this part of Kent. And I told her something I'd never really told anyone before: that I was sure I could read people, especially their energy and intentions. I told her I'd been picking up and absorbing bad vibes every day since I'd moved here.

'I think this is telling me that you're ready for a great transformation in your life,' Odelia said. 'You need to create change in your world and the world around you.'

She gently talked to me about the judgement she'd heard when I'd explained the lay of the land I was living in; however, she also instantly understood where I was coming from.

'I think this stone is telling you that you need to see the connection to spirit in everything. Even the shit stuff, you know?' she said. 'You're living in a world full of intellectual people. People who think they know it all. And that's okay. That doesn't make them bad people. It actually makes them a bit like you. You're a thinker. A doer. An analyser of words and information.'

She'd got it in one – I knew that I was judging people and I hated myself for it. I knew I needed to move beyond thinking that everything was a potential problem and see the world I lived in as something that could happily evolve.

'I think that you're a bridge. An alchemist,' Odelia went on. 'Your purpose might well be to share the things you've learnt with these people in a way that they can understand, because you're actually a bit like them... you get it.'

Suddenly, it made sense. This was like therapy. Maybe my discomfort was my power. Maybe this was the exact reason I'd started this spiritual journey surrounded by people who didn't seem to be on my wavelength. It was all part of the process. I was fighting against something that was also a part of me. Maybe I *could* be a bridge.

'There are enough people in the spiritual world being super-connected goddesses who live life to its highest purpose,' Odelia continued. 'There aren't enough people who can connect across the divide and show sceptics the positive potential of some of these practices. I really think you need to write more about this.'

I liked her thinking.

It was time to devise a question for the second crystal in the reading: 'What's going to help me with this challenge?' A stone jumped out at me straight away. I'd never seen anything like it before: Shiva lingam. A river stone. A stone about balance and rebirth and connecting to the inner child. I was so excited, I started taking notes again. Odelia told me to stop.

'You're a mother,' she said. 'And I think I can tell that you're a great mother. You play, you talk, you allow them to feel what they feel.'

'Of course,' I said.

'Well, what about you? What about your inner child? Do you allow yourself to play and move and be silly and feel?'

'Erm, no!' I said quickly.

'This is what this stone is telling you. Stop the judgement. Stop the thinking. Start feeling. You're not lacking heart, but you need to mix it up!'

'I have literally never thought about any of this before,' I replied. 'I've definitely never given my inner child a second thought.'

'Well, now is the time,' Odelia replied. 'In order to transform, in order to be this bridge you're here to be, you need to enjoy it more. Enjoy the process. See the connections to spirit in everything.'

I felt buoyant. I liked what she was saying. No one had ever told me to indulge myself and just have fun. Why did it feel like such a revelation? Wasn't that the whole reason I'd started this project – to get back in touch with the witchy child who had found magic in the moon and the stars? Wasn't I meant to be finding inner peace and making life more magical? Why did I need to turn everything into a blog post or a project? Why did I have to overthink it all?

It was time for the final question: 'Let's say you learn the lessons,' Odelia said. 'You become this alchemist, this bridge. You learn to play and have fun and be silly and move. What energy would it bring to you?'

I couldn't choose between two crystals – citrine and another stone I'd never seen before, larimar. I was still trying to decide when Odelia went with both. 'Citrine could not be more perfect for you,' she said. 'It's the stone you want to get when you ask about your future. It's also related to amethyst, your first stone, and I love that.'

Then she explained that this crystal showed that if I learnt the lessons I needed to, great abundance would await me. Citrine is power and positivity and inner strength. If I could become the bridge, be the alchemist and get down with my much-neglected inner child, who knew what wonders were awaiting me.

'I think that when you really open up to the beauty of the universe and really see that we're all connected, things will start to make more sense for you,' Odelia continued.

I told her about my reiki treatment with Myra two weeks earlier, and how I'd felt something like that during it. It really did feel as if Odelia was reading my mind. Or seeing into my soul. Or just making connections that I hadn't yet been able to make.

'Let's do the other stone,' she said. 'Larimar – a rare and special stone connected to the throat chakra and the energy of the sea and dolphins.'

'I know why I've chosen this one,' I said. 'I'm a Pisces and the sea is my happy place. I'm going to Greece with my family in a few days' time. When you mentioned playfulness earlier, I instantly saw myself playing in the sea with my children.'

'I think you're right,' she replied. 'I think it's another sign that you need to release judgement and build this bridge. And really connect to the sea more if it makes you happy.'

Odelia suggested I meditate with sea sounds or dolphin sounds. She reminded me that although dolphins play they're also very intelligent. Almost like bridges themselves. I could feel the stress seeping out of me as I visualized myself on a beach in Greece – unstressed by deadlines and work decisions and just playing with my girls, soaking up the sea, and living in the moment for once in my life.

Perhaps the change I needed most really was right in front of me, waiting for me to just allow it to happen. I decided there and then to let it be, to take those weeks off to just be a mother and a wife and a daughter and a friend – to just be me.

In 50 minutes Odelia and her crystals had cracked the code. She hadn't just helped me decide what my next step in life should be – she'd also helped reframe the way I thought about crystals. Crystal healing wasn't hocus-pocus after all, and there was a lot more to it than just sticking a piece of pyrite in your purse and waiting for a windfall.

Chosen intuitively and used as a guidance tool, crystals offered something that I definitely wanted in on.

For me, when used in combination with the right questions and space for exploration, crystals were life-changing. Later that day I looked up the meaning of my green moonstone: calm, reflection, going with the flow, emotional healing, insight, peace, connection.

All the things I'd been seeking when I picked it out in March. Crystals really did make sense after all.

Do it yourself – power up with crystals

If you'd like to use crystals intuitively, simply allow yourself to be drawn to a particular stone before referring to its properties and meaning. Lay out your stones (if you have some at home) and pick one without overthinking it. If you don't yet have any crystals you could do the same by scrolling through an online selection, heading for a display in a local crystal shop or flicking through an illustrated guidebook. Check out the below to discover what your chosen crystal might be trying to tell you.

Rose quartz – You may need more love or self-love in your life

Amethyst – You may need to slow down, tune in or call time on an unhealthy habit

Black tourmaline – You may be feeling overwhelmed and in need of protection right now

Pyrite – You're feeling ready to take your life to the next level, manifest some magic and invite in all the abundance

Tiger's eye – It's time to believe in yourself more and turn that creative idea into something real

Moonstone – You may be ignoring a niggling feeling that needs your attention

Citrine – You're ready for some good vibes and positivity to come your way

Smoky quartz – It's time to kick some negative energy to the kerb and start showing up for yourself again

Crystal fixes

Once you've chosen a crystal to work with there are a few things you can do to super-charge its powers. Crystals are thought to absorb energy from the world around them so giving yours a cleansing refresh before you ask it to help you with an intention or a goal makes sense. And we've all seen the memes about charging crystals and full moons, right? Charging a crystal is said to power it up for extra good vibes. Do both and you'll be ready to activate your new partner in crime.

See below for tips and suggestions. Note that some crystals, like selenite, don't fare well in water, so check before you immerse them!

Cleanse

You can clear a crystal's energy by:

- Holding it under running water

- Immersing it in salt water

- Burning herbs or lighting incense and allowing the smoke to waft over it

- Spritzing an aura spray or mist over it

- Visualizing it surrounded by white light

Charge

You can give a crystal a power boost by:

- Letting it soak up some sunshine

- Leaving it out in the moonlight

- Putting it on a selenite crystal charging plate

- Placing it upon the Earth

Activate

Make your crystal work for you by:

- Putting it under your pillow with a list of wishes

- Holding it in your hand as you speak your goal, intention or wish aloud

- Asking it how it can help you in meditation

- Carrying it with you for luck

August

WRITTEN IN THE STARS

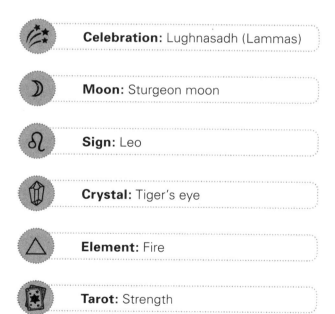

Celebration: Lughnasadh (Lammas)

Moon: Sturgeon moon

Sign: Leo

Crystal: Tiger's eye

Element: Fire

Tarot: Strength

Stargazing with sceptics

'I don't believe in astrology. I'm a
Sagittarius and we're sceptical.'

ARTHUR C. CLARKE

If you've recently reignited your love of astrology to the point
that it's all you want to talk about after a couple of rosés, can I
recommend that you don't go on holiday with an astrophysicist?
They put a real downer on the whole thing.

It was August and we were in Skiathos, Greece, about to top off
an evening of sunsets, sea views and excessive feta consumption
with a bit of low-key postprandial astrology. My husband Alexis (a
classic Leo) is half Greek and we spend every summer with his
family on the small island that's seen him celebrate every single
one of his August birthdays.

My work as a freelance writer allows me to digital-nomad-it-up for
a few weeks with my laptop (and the kids) while Alexis flies out
for a swift fortnight the second his NHS work will allow. Doting
grandparents to help with the children, beautiful beaches and
sunshine on tap – it's a total no-brainer. And don't worry: I really
do know how lucky I am.

Even before my mystical year, the wonder of weeks spent
watching the sun rise and set and the moon wax and wane
was never lost on me. With its big-sky views and pine-scented
air, Skiathos is a place where the magic of the cosmos is right
there above you, stretching out to a watery horizon. It's a place
where stars really do shoot across the sky as you gaze up at
the midnight heavens. A place where golden-hour sunsets cast

chilled-out faces in a magical glow. A place where life happens outside, in nature and in tune with nature – like one long exhale in the sunshine.

It's also the ideal setting to encourage a few friends to look beyond the star sign basics with some moon and rising sign home truths... or so I thought. I was just explaining how an Aries rising sign might explain the fiery, go-getting side of an otherwise dreamy Piscean personality when the aforementioned astrophysicist – Richie, Alexis's Physics master's lab partner and best man at our wedding – piped up with an exasperated, 'It's all total rubbish, you know!' Such a Capricorn. Such a scientist.

The thing is, I'm totally here for the science bit. I'm happy to listen to facts about the planets in our solar system being too far away to possibly impact life on Earth. Or the thing about the constellations being in different positions today to those they were in when the zodiac was created. I quite like it when that 'NASA declares 13th star sign' revelation comes round every few years. I particularly enjoy the idea that NASA has nothing better to do than ponder the inaccuracies of astrology.

I understand that sun sign astrology (the horoscopes we all know and love) reduces the world's people to 12 different types and that every Scorpio on the planet can't possibly have a big windfall on the same day. I don't need to be a scientist to know that astrology isn't scientific. Or that at times, its very existence makes some people (particularly scientists!) spectacularly angry. But at the end of the day, I don't really care. And I doubt whether many other astro aficionados do either.

If I needed overwhelming evidence and a double-blind large-sample study before letting something become part of my life, I really wouldn't be writing this book. I'm not anti-science by any means – that would be ridiculous – I just don't think everything in life needs to be quantified before its value can be ascertained.

I became obsessed with astrology from the moment I learnt what my star sign was and what that was meant to stand for. The description of Pisces was quite simply me. Through and through. And when I read about the star signs (also known as sun signs) of my friends and family, I saw them in the descriptions too. As far as I'm concerned, astrology transcends logic for all the right reasons.

> *Astrology holds up a big cosmic mirror that reflects back all sorts of magic, mystery and ancient wisdom.*

It offers a framework for understanding what makes us tick. And what makes other people tick, too. It's insightful, it's flawed, it's the whole damned rainbow. And who wants to live their life in black and white?

For me, astrology has long been a valuable guidance tool, a way to become more self-aware and more aware of the people around me. It's yet another gift from the ancient world that makes a whole lot of sense in the modern one. People have looked to the skies to help plan their lives for thousands of years, whether that was seafaring voyagers following the North Star home or Inca farmers looking to the star cluster Pleiades to predict the abundance of the coming harvest.

The foundations of Western astrology were laid by the ancient Babylonians, who divided the sky into different constellations, and later the ancient Greeks, who rationalized the 'zodiac' (meaning circle of animals) into the signs and symbolism we use in astrology today. And, man, how we love those symbols.

Are you a secretive Scorpio with a sting in your tail? Or a perfectionist Virgo who likes everything to be just so? Perhaps you're a mystical Piscean who's happiest swimming around the dream world inside your own head? Or a go-getting Capricorn with a razor-sharp focus on building your empire?

Most of us know what our star sign is and most of us, to some extent, find we can relate to the classic characteristics that astrology suggests belong to that sign. We see ourselves. And we get it. Which is exactly what makes horoscopes so much fun. The flashes of recognition. The confidence boosts. The call-outs. The starry explanations for the way you are that make you feel understood and just a little bit better about being you. I'll never not love opening a magazine horoscope column and turning to the part that says Pisces.

Yet astrology is so much more than just star signs, which is exactly why I was trying to engage my Greek island dinner guests in a bit of deeper astro exploration. Ever since Odelia and her crystals had told me that I was a bridge, I'd been trying to think of ways to share the mystical adventures I'd found most insightful with the people I cared about. I knew I wasn't about to change the world with some late-night chat about rising signs but it felt like a decent enough place to start. I knew from experience that even the smallest of scratches beneath the sun sign surface had the potential to initiate a whole host of cosmic light-bulb moments.

Of course, I haven't always been quite so engrossed in the finer points of the cosmos. Astrology once meant little more to me than checking out my horoscope (and that of the current object of my desire) and trying to read a romantic Saturday night interlude into whatever I found there. Way back when, I was all about the teen mag stars pages, watching astrologer Russell Grant on breakfast television and, later, a book called *Suzanne White's Guide to Love* that I used as a sort of romantic bible. But once I delved a little deeper, there was no going back.

I first had my birth chart read by mail order in the late 1990s. I can't remember how much it cost, but I do remember the day it landed on the doormat of my student house in Liverpool. And I definitely remember how it felt to open that envelope and feel seen. So, *that's* why I'm like this! It all made so much sense!

As a typical dreamy, creative Piscean, my behind-the-scenes desire for stability and security never felt like something that fitted – until I discovered my Taurus moon sign. Of course! Taureans are all about strong foundations and beautiful things! And moon signs reveal our emotional inner selves and what we need to feel secure. Perhaps this explained why I always found it so hard to focus on work or be creative if my home life was up in the air.

It was the same when I discovered my rising sign (also known as the ascendant), Virgo. This is where a mother with a good memory comes in handy because rising signs – which reveal the way we present ourselves to the world – change every couple of hours. I actually spent a while thinking my ascendant was Libra due to a birth time memory mix-up with my sister – but once you discover yours, it's quite the revelation.

Rising signs explain how we might be perceived by others and mine made so much sense. I'd long been baffled when people told me how together I was, how organized I was, how I knew what I was doing – all classic Virgo traits that I didn't feel applied to the chaotic Piscean world inside my mind. It also helped explain my need to analyse everything to excess and the perfectionist streak that gave me palpitations every time I handed in an essay or filed a magazine feature. And those two examples were just the tip of the birth-chart iceberg.

> ✧ *The deeper I delved into astrology the better I understood who I was and what my potential could be. It was like a roadmap for life.*

It made me consider aspects of my personality I'd never paid attention to before. It gave me the confidence to believe in myself. It also made me wonder how much I could learn about my friends, my family and annoying ex-boyfriends if I just persuaded them to hand over their date, time and place of birth.

But back to August in Greece and my sceptical friend trying to mind his own business with a game of backgammon on the balcony... I poured another round of drinks, booted up my laptop and got to work looking up chart placements for everyone who was showing an interest.

I looked up moon signs to reveal inner selves. Rising signs for public selves. Venus signs for relationship styles. And midheavens (or MC) for clues about career aspirations and life purpose. Soon the children and their friends were clamouring for turns. Then, Richie's wife Lucy was calling him over: 'This stuff is good, you know!'

I wasn't doing 'proper astrology' by any stretch. I wasn't delivering much detail or even taking it particularly seriously, but the magic was there all the same. I saw it in the quiet gasps of recognition. In the kid hollering 'I'm a lion!' as he roared into the pine forest surrounding the villa. In the 'Yes! That *is* me!' moments that just kept coming. And I could definitely see it in the instant desire for more, more, more. That's the thing about astrology: it's all about *you*. And once you start getting into it, it can be very hard to stop. Even if you're an astrophysicist.

Do it yourself – seek solace in the stars

Are you an astrology super-fan already? If you are, I know you get it! You never stop learning with astrology – that's the magic of it. There's always something to read into more deeply or a new flashing light-bulb moment when you check out a birth chart or dive into a transit.

The great thing about getting to grips with astrology is that it enables us to understand more than just ourselves. Check out the birth charts of the people closest to you and you'll soon see the life-changing power of astrology in action. Perhaps your shy, secretive sibling who never opens up has a mysterious Scorpio moon? Perhaps your radical activist mate relates more to her Aquarius rising than she does her Pisces sun?

Look into those connection-at-first-sight friends and lovers and you'll be amazed by how many have a moon sign that matches your sun or vice versa. Tap into the magic of astrology, even just a little bit, and you'll soon find yourself one step closer to making your world a more magical and harmonious place.

Discover your birth chart

Discovering the secrets of your birth chart (which is a snapshot of the sky at the moment you were born) can feel like cracking a secret code. And the good news is that doing so is easier than ever – you no longer have to send off a stamped addressed envelope and wait 14 days for it to wing its way back to you by mail, for starters!

You could book yourself a session with an astrologer, plug your birth details into an online astro site like Astro.com, Astro Seek or Café Astrology, read *The Signs*, Carolyne Faulkner's brilliantly accessible guide to understanding your chart, or simply download an app on your phone. (See the August entry in the Spiritual Sourcebook for more information).

You'll get a different level of depth and insight depending on what you opt for, but that's not necessarily a bad thing. Astrology is a complicated business and trying to get to grips with all of it at the same time is one hell of an undertaking. You really don't need to understand everything in intricate detail right this moment (or ever!) to gain some truly valuable cosmic insights.

Look beyond your star sign

If you've never delved deeper than your horoscope before, brace yourself, because there are revelations galore in moon signs and rising signs, planets and houses and all the other celestial bodies in on the act.

I love horoscopes so much that I write them every month for *Glamour UK*, but I know that astrology has so much more to offer if you go even a tiny bit deeper. Below are speed-readings for some of my favourite enlightening astro placements if you fancy kick-starting your own journey of zodiac discovery. They're just a taster, and just for fun, but who knows where it might lead?

Your moon sign

The moon changes astrological sign every couple of days so you should be able to find out what your moon sign is, even if you don't know what time you were born. Your moon sign represents your inner, emotional self and what you *really need* to feel secure in life.

Moon in Aries – Boredom is soul-destroying for you. You like life high-vibe, high-energy and full of excitement. And you want to go first.

Moon in Taurus – You have a deep need for stability. You like to enjoy the finer things in life. Find the solid foundation you crave and you'll reach for the stars.

Moon in Gemini – You need to talk. A lot. New ideas make your heart beat faster with excitement. Life feels right when it's fresh and fun and you're right in the middle of the action.

Moon in Cancer – For you, home is where the heart is. Above all else you need to feel truly loved and secure. You sometimes get lost in nostalgia at the expense of living in the now.

Moon in Leo – There's not much you like more than an audience. You need to feel seen. You like your life on the glamorous side. And you love being generous. You don't love the drama – it loves you.

Moon in Virgo – You're happiest with your ducks in a row. You need to feel that you're making a difference. If there's a problem, you can't help but want to find a way to solve it.

Moon in Libra – It's all about the inner (and outer) peace for you. You're happiest when life feels harmonious and everyone's getting on. You're even happier if you know your look is on point at the same time.

Moon in Scorpio – There's nothing superficial about you, and you're not as calm as you look. You're a deep thinker who needs to feel understood. Your loyalty means you'll take a secret to the grave.

Moon in Sagittarius – A passport and a plane ticket and you're happy. You need constant stimulation, adventure, and friends who can handle your tell-it-like-it-is honesty.

Moon in Capricorn – You have a deep need to succeed. You're happiest when your empire is growing and your goals are being well and truly smashed.

Moon in Aquarius – You need a mission in life. You love a crusade and are always ready to stick it to The Man. Above all, you need to feel free to be happy.

Moon in Pisces – You were born to create. You need time to daydream. You're happiest when life gives you space to enjoy the world inside your own head.

Your rising sign

Your rising sign represents your public self – the *you* that you present to the world, the *you* that others see. You'll need a fairly accurate birth time (within a couple of hours) for this one and it's worth trying to find it out. Some people discover that they relate more closely to their rising sign than their star sign. Next time you check out your horoscope try reading what's been written for your rising sign as well as your sun sign.

How other people perceive you…

Aries rising – Quick-witted, go-getting, fast-paced rebel

Taurus rising – Reliable, strong-willed, lover of the good life

Gemini rising – Super smart, quick-witted chatterbox

Cancer rising – A lover, a nurturer and a good friend in a crisis

Leo rising – A confident fun-lover who stands out in a crowd

Virgo rising – Organized and totally together with a side order of earth mother

Libra rising – An indecisive charmer with good intentions

Scorpio rising – Magical, mysterious and irresistibly sexy

Sagittarius rising – An outspoken optimist with a lust for life's great adventures

Capricorn rising – Powerful, driven and definitely going places

Aquarius rising – A clever, one-of-a-kind crusader on a mission

Pisces rising – Head in the clouds, flaky dreamer for life

Your Venus sign

Venus is the planet of love and beauty and your Venus sign reveals the placement of this planet at the time you were born. Venus typically stays in a sign for around 30 days (with some variation) so you can discover this one without an accurate birth time. Your Venus sign represents your romantic needs and the way you approach love.

Venus in Aries – You want it all and you want it now. You fall hard and fast and believe in love at first sight. When you say what you want, you usually get it.

Venus in Taurus – Love often lands in your lap. You might take time to warm up in a relationship but you're all about the romance. You believe in the power of seduction.

Venus in Gemini – You take flirtation to the next level. And you like to keep things interesting in a relationship. You're difficult to tie down and prone to wandering eyes!

Venus in Cancer – You're a nostalgic homebody on a mission to find The One. You give a lot of yourself in a relationship. Definitely the marrying kind.

Venus in Leo – You're a thrill-seeker who loves the chase (and the drama) but are hopelessly devoted once you find the right person. You like to spoil the object of your desire.

Venus in Virgo – You're more practical than poetic, but you're ready to commit to the right person. Not easily swayed by traditional 'romance', you're looking for someone who loves the natural world as much as you do.

Venus in Libra – A serial monogamist who likes to seduce and be seduced the old-fashioned way. Basically, you love love, you love romance and you love being part of a harmonious pair.

Venus in Scorpio – You're super intense and magnetically attractive. But you're not one for meaningless flings. People can't help but be drawn to you. You're never not keeping some sort of secret.

Venus in Sagittarius – You like to think big in life and love, and are always ready for an adventure. You're the sign most likely to run away for romance and thrive in relationships where you are able to feel free.

Venus in Capricorn – You're ready to be part of a power couple and aren't afraid of commitment. You have high expectations when it comes to love and aim for the stars in all areas of life.

Venus in Aquarius – Often happily single but willing to experiment. Not bothered about tradition or societal expectations. Above all, you want to feel in charge of your own destiny and free to be yourself.

Venus in Pisces – You're a romantic idealist who can make anyone fall in love with you. And it doesn't take much for you to love them right back. Shame your fantasy doesn't always match up with reality.

Your midheaven

Marked 'MC' on a birth chart, the midheaven is another cosmic big reveal for which you need an accurate birth time. Your MC offers insights into how you might find success and what your life's purpose or legacy might be.

Aries midheaven – You'll find success by getting there first. Your ideas might seem radical to some but be brave enough to follow them through and you'll be unstoppable.

Taurus midheaven – You're here to build something from the ground up. Your legacy will take time but it will be steadfast and strong and make the world a more beautiful place.

Gemini midheaven – You're destined to share a big idea with an impressively large audience. When you talk, people listen – and you definitely have something to say.

Cancer midheaven – Your legacy might well be your family or bringing groups of people together. You're on a caring mission for connection and good.

Leo midheaven – You're here to shine in the spotlight and let the good times roll. Your legacy could be your big-hearted generosity towards a cause, a project or a person you care about.

Virgo midheaven – You're here to make the world a better place by solving problems in a new way. You're always willing to work hard and have a knack for explaining complex issues in a way that anyone can understand.

Libra midheaven – You're here to make connections, smooth ruffled feathers and build others up. You have the power to bring people together to create positive change.

Scorpio midheaven – You're here to smash taboos and to cut to the chase. Your legacy could involve understanding power and influence and knowing when and how to break those things down.

Sagittarius midheaven – You're here to learn, adapt and adventure – and take others along for the ride. Your legacy may be your bravery and speaking your truth.

Capricorn midheaven – Your legacy is your empire and building it is your mission. You were born to blaze a trail and succeed.

Aquarius midheaven – You're not here to be labelled or told what your legacy might be. You're here to be yourself, to make connections and to think outside the box with a life-changing idea.

Pisces midheaven – You're here to share your imagination and idealistic dreams with the world. Your legacy may involve creating something or making a difference through your kindness, compassion and imagination.

Septem ber

EMPATHS, INTUITION & INDECISION

Celebration: Mabon (autumn equinox)

Moon: Harvest moon

Sign: Virgo

Crystal: Sapphire

Element: Earth

Tarot: The Hermit

Feeling feelings

'Of course I feel too much. I am a
universe of exploding stars.'

SARA AJNA

The summer wasn't all sunsets and stargazing and cosmic balcony revelations. There were tough times, too. August began with the first anniversary of my father-in-law John's death. So much had happened in the 365 days since the sun first rose without him. So much had changed since his big Catholic funeral at the end of that strange, sad month the year before. When I thought back to how I'd felt at the beginning of September 2017, it was like remembering a different person.

I'm not sure whether 2018 me would have hotfooted it to Norfolk for a friend's 40th birthday weekend the morning after a family funeral, but that's what 2017 me did. One minute I was raising a glass to a black-and-white photo montage set to Tom Petty's 'Wildflowers' at the wake in John's local pub, the Windsor Castle, the next I was hurtling round the M25 in the back of my friend Fiona's VW estate.

'How was it?' Fiona's husband James asked from the driving seat as I slumped across the back seat.

'Pretty awful,' I replied. 'And also amazing. It's hard to explain. It was such a huge turnout. So many people. Such a big life. Man, I'm actually done in.'

'I think we need to stop for supplies,' said Fiona. She's a life coach, so she knows when not to push a topic any further. 'I'm getting you a Diet Coke and some crisps.'

'Thanks,' I said weakly.

It was a good job I pre-hydrated with that Diet Coke because the moment we arrived, I launched myself at the prosecco. Usually I try to be careful about my alcohol intake, but that weekend I just didn't care. The birthday girl, my childhood friend Sarah, used to work in events and she'd catered for cocktails as if she was running the backstage bar at Glastonbury Festival. There were margaritas and cosmopolitans and negronis and booze-fuelled afternoon teas, and I wasn't planning to say no to any of it.

All the guests had chipped in for the hire of a rambling country house with a hot tub, a dubious-looking swimming pool and a sweeping driveway that led to a grand entrance bookended by inflatable birthday unicorns. Sarah was sharing the celebrations with her friend Kat, so there were people to meet and friends to make and distractions galore. By the time Alexis joined us a day later, I'd stashed the funeral order of service with his father's face on the front at the bottom of an overnight bag. Out of sight, out of mind. This weekend was the perfect escape from reality and that was exactly what I was looking for.

To be more precise: I was looking for oblivion. I wanted to feel nothing at all. I drained one glass and then another and another until my bloodstream flooded with something that felt like relief. Mind-numbing self-medication. Thoughts eclipsed by silence. Feeling nothing was what I needed because up until then I'd been feeling *everything*.

I'm going to take a guess that you might be able to relate to this. Have you ever been told you're too sensitive? Or that you think too much? Have you ever felt so strung out by big emotions that you just want to obliterate them with whatever tools (wine, maybe) you have to hand? Do you ever get the sense that some of the feelings you have don't really belong to you – as if you're carrying someone else's burden around? Do you identify a bit too strongly with tragic leads in tragic films? Do people always want to tell you their life story?

Have you heard of the term empath? I hadn't. I've always known that I'm someone who can read people. I've been able to sense the energy in a room since I was a child. I've long found other people's bad moods or unhappiness difficult to deal with. And often I think that it's all my fault. How can it not be? I feel terrible, so I must be responsible!

I knew what empathy was but I didn't know that if you ditched the 'y' it became a word that could explain a complicated part of who I was – until I found myself typing things like 'Am I too sensitive?' into Google a few weeks after the funeral and that raucous milestone birthday party. Back-to-back events that left me with the kind of hangover that doesn't disappear after a couple of paracetamol and a few early nights.

It's said that an empath is someone who is so attuned to other people's perspectives that they can feel others' feelings as if they were their own. I'd write that off as self-indulgent rubbish if I didn't know in my oversensitive bones that it's true.

 Empaths are emotional sponges. They get people. They read rooms. They care too much. They feel too much. They're easily overwhelmed.

Sometimes, empaths absorb other people's feelings to the extent that those feelings manifest all over again within their own body. And sometimes that manifestation physically hurts.

Delays to the funeral meant there were three weeks between my father-in-law's death and the celebration of the life he'd lived. My husband and I were out in Skiathos with our girls when the sad news arrived and the rest of his family soon joined us to wait it out.

A quiet melancholy settled over the house that had been the scene of many a magical summer as we all tried to make the best of a very bad situation. And as the only adult non-immediate family member in the mix, I knew I had to step up to the plate. I distracted the children (my own and my sister-in-law Phaedra's). I rewrote clumsily worded obituaries. I poured drinks. I listened. I soaked it all in.

I turned myself into a shock absorber, a go-between, a hawk-eyed observer of fractious energy. I was ready to pounce on triggers and smooth out cracks before they could even appear. I didn't do any of this because I was asked to (I wasn't) — I did it because I wanted to. I was a long way down the hierarchy of grief but John was my daughters' grandfather. And these were my people.

He hadn't been a faultless man but we all loved him. I also did it because I didn't know any other way. Fix it. Mend it. Make it better. Be the light in the storm. It didn't occur to me that the people around me might not even want a light right now. Or that it was actually acceptable for this particular life event to just be plain horrendous.

By the time the date of our flight home arrived I felt ill and exhausted, and I had a headache that wouldn't go away, no matter how many pills I popped. The life–work–home pressures I'd already been struggling to deal with in 2017 felt stupid and irrelevant now, but they didn't just disappear. If anything, they added fuel to the fire.

And by the day of the funeral, I was pouring Bach's Rescue Remedy into my mouth like it was water. I was falling apart when I needed to be strong for the people I cared about. I focused on my girls, plaiting hair with shaking hands and whispering platitudes into tiny ears across funeral-car back seats.

At the wake, I watched on, detached. Black-and-white photos of a life well lived, snapshots of self-made success; an Armani-clad architect; a powerhouse of charisma; a generous man who really wouldn't have wanted to leave the party so soon. Pictures of boats and beaches and buildings, of friends and family and good times. There were so many people in that room. So many memories. So much to absorb.

Funerals are peculiar things – the complexities of a multifaceted life brushed aside for a tear-jerking highlight reel. Commiserations and contradictions. Regrets revealed. Meaning refracted by other people's perceptions of what happened when and why. Secrets hidden behind smiles. The strangest mix of memory and legend, melancholy and joy.

I knew that John's impact on the people closest to him hadn't always been sunshine and rainbows, but you're not allowed to think about the bad bits at a funeral. So I soaked it all up and stored it within myself. Until I could drown it in 40th birthday party oblivion.

By the time life got back to a strangely staggered normal, I was on the verge of collapse. Alexis went back to work at the hospital. The kids settled in for the last week of the summer holidays. And I pretty much went to bed. I made my girls breakfast and then I lay down again. I took them to the park and then I lay down again. If I could get away with it, I stayed horizontal, motionless and silent until something forced me to move. I felt broken.

I didn't tell a soul because I didn't think I had the right to feel the way I did. He wasn't *my* dad. Who did I think I was? I also didn't realize then that what I was feeling wasn't mine alone to bear. The grief. The sadness. The shock. The anger. The strange disconnect between the reality of a life and the soft-focus glow cast over the posthumous version. It wasn't until I started researching empaths that it all clicked into place. Maybe this clicks something into place for you, too?

Being an empath isn't a diagnosis you can get by making an appointment with your GP. And if I'm honest, there was something about the idea of taking on the label empath – even just privately to myself – that made me cringe. Feeling awkward about it didn't make it any less real, though. I knew it was true. And I knew I couldn't possibly be the only one.

Many of us are used to carrying burdens that are greater than our own. How many times have you found yourself rushing in to smooth ruffled feathers because seeing them out of place ruffles *you*? How often have you found yourself taking someone else's emotional reaction deep into your heart and holding it there? How often do you put other people's needs, thoughts and feelings before your own? Or take on those feelings as if they're yours to fix?

Maybe you don't need to answer that. Maybe you already know. If you're a sensitive soul who also has children, I'm doubly sure you don't need me to tell you what it means to be an empath. When author Sarah Payne Stuart said that 'You are only as happy as your least happy child' was the best description of parenthood she'd ever read, I think she hit the nail on the head. It's tough out there when you feel too much.

Being an empath may be a self-identifying affair, but how do you decide if you *are* one? According to Judith Orloff, author of *The Empath's Survival Guide*, there are numerous signs. Her book has a self-assessment questionnaire called 'Are you an empath?' that asks readers to answer yes or no to a series of questions about, among many other things, being labelled by others as overly sensitive or introverted, regularly feeling anxious or overwhelmed, sensing that you don't fit in, feeling ill after arguments, needing to leave social situations early, and finding multitasking overwhelming. The more questions to which you answer yes, the more of an empath you are.

When a friend went through that questionnaire with me over drinks in that sad autumn of 2017, I wasn't at all surprised to find I responded yes to nearly all the questions. I'd long felt overwhelmed by many of the things Orloff mentioned in her list. And I knew it was high time I found a way to fix it. I mean, how hard could it be? Pretty damned hard, as it turned out.

I tried and failed and tried again. It seemed this wasn't a switch that could simply be turned off. Understanding what an empath was had helped me to see what I was dealing with, but actually dealing with it was a whole different matter. I began to wonder if I'd just been born this way.

It wasn't until later, right in the middle of my mystical year, that I discovered this might actually be true. I'd assumed this was a problem that was mostly about other people. Being an empath affected me on a personal level, but surely I could control it if I just tried harder – if I somehow managed to change my interactions with the world around me?

Discovering that there might be a genetic element to empathy made me think again. A 2018 study by scientists at the UK's University of Cambridge found that around 10 per cent of the difference in how empathetic people are is down to genetics.

Maybe I really had been born this way. Was it even possible to fix that part, and should I want to?

Whether being an empath is nature, nurture, or something in between, I'd finally arrived at a plan of action. I decided to put together my second mystical toolkit of the year, but this time there wouldn't be much shopping involved. I just needed some easy techniques to help me navigate the onslaught of overwhelm that came with feeling those blasted feelings. Spiritual hygiene, protecting my energy, tricks of the empath trade – I was on the hunt for answers and I wanted them fast.

Do it yourself – mystical toolkit #2 (the empath version)

You'll find all sorts of advice, ideas and information online if you're interested in delving deeper into the subject of empaths, but here are a few of the mystical techniques I discovered worked for me.

Let's go outside

Sometimes you just need to create some space and there's no better place to do that than the great outdoors. Don't think that you need to have a national beauty spot on your doorstep to benefit, either. Simply shutting the front door behind you and breathing in and out for five minutes can be enough of a reset when times get tough in empath world. I'm pretty sure everything feels better outside of four walls.

Visualization

Try some positive visualization. Imagine every cell in your body being flooded with protective white light – a light that forms a force field around you that nothing and no one can penetrate. This is a commonly used technique in spiritual practice, so if you want to be guided through a visualization you'll find all sorts of iterations of this theme online.

Get grounded

When everything feels as if it's out of control, it helps to get grounded. For me, one of the best ways to do this is to simply walk barefoot on the Earth (admittedly, this isn't always the most appealing option when you're at the mercy of the British weather). Consciously sense the ground beneath your feet as you take slow, deliberate steps, feeling the solid stability of the Earth underfoot.

And if you don't fancy stepping outside, a salt bath can also do the trick (see Mystical Toolkit #1 in the March chapter). Immersing yourself in water is a brilliantly relaxing way to let go of energy and feelings that don't belong to you.

Quick fixes

Sometimes it's an emergency. Sometimes you don't have time for a hot bath or a barefoot stroll or a white-light visualization. Sometimes you need a reset and you need it now. That's where adding some quick fixes to your toolkit comes in.

Try stashing a protective crystal in your pocket (black tourmaline is said to have grounding, stabilizing qualities) and giving it a squeeze when you need an energetic boost. Or keep an aura spray to hand for spritzing spaces and/or yourself whenever you need to banish bad vibes.

Better boundaries

This is the big one, and the hardest to crack. Practise saying no. See what happens if, sometimes, you allow yourself to take rather than give. Try to be brave enough to admit that you need space or time alone, or for someone to stop using you as a sounding board for all their problems. I can't say that I'm 100 per cent there with protecting my energy in this way yet, but I'm working on it.

If learning how to protect your energy is the first step towards coping with life as an empath, the second step is realizing that it isn't necessarily a bad thing to be one. It might not feel that way when you're dealing with anxiety and stress and overwhelm, but being an empath can also be incredibly powerful.

Signs that you might be an empath

Here's how to tell:

♦   You're highly sensitive

♦   You're easily overwhelmed

♦   You need to spend time alone to reboot

♦   You feel what other people are feeling

♦   You feel as if you need to fix things

♦   You feel like you're always giving

♦   You become exhausted by large groups

- ◆ You can read the energy of a room

- ◆ You know what other people are thinking

In my experience, being an empath means seeing things as they really are. Empaths often know instinctively when people are lying. And they're also able to tune in to how other people really feel.

If you can relate to this, you may have experienced these things for yourself. Perhaps you pick up on things that other people don't. Or you see the secrets behind the story – the dangerous intentions hidden in a glance across a crowded room; the false friendship built on toxic wants or plans for personal gain.

You get it. You know it. You feel it deep within you. And once you've learnt how to separate what belongs to you and what doesn't, you might also find you have the most incredible, almost psychic, intuition. And in that perhaps you'll find another kind of power.

Tune in (and decide already)

'Intuition is the GPS of the soul.'
ANON

When I wasn't casting my mind back to the ghosts of Septembers past and trying to keep my empath issues in check, I was having a pretty good time. I've always been a sucker for that fresh, back-to-school feeling you get when the air turns crisp.

Normally in September, I'd be chomping at the bit to pack my kids off to school so I could catch up with all the work teetering dangerously on the back burner, but this year was different. I didn't have that much to do. I had three Greek hotel reviews to send off to the travel section of a newspaper and, well, nothing else – bar becoming that bridge that Odelia and her crystals had told me about.

I'd never really stepped off the hamster wheel of modern life for so long before. And it felt good. I took myself off on autumnal walks and said yes when friends wanted to meet for coffee. I started entertaining wholesome family-life fantasies featuring butternut squash recipes that made my kids cry and beg for oven chips. I broke the washing machine while attempting to get on top of the laundry mountain once and for all. I upped my yoga game to two classes a week.

I read books that had been gathering dust on my bedside table for months. I remembered birthdays and wrote to my grandma and felt grateful every day without having to set a reminder for it on my phone. I knew I was lucky to be able to do this – to take my foot ever-so-slightly off the gas for a while.

 I'd created space in my life and I was leaving the universe in charge of filling it with something that was right for me.

The trouble was, I just couldn't work out how I was meant to know when that right thing came knocking. I'd spent a lot of time since the year began trying to tune in to my inner voice and intuition, but when it came to this particular life–work–future situation, it seemed strangely quiet. Either that, or I just couldn't hear it above the noise. The clawing, anxious feeling that kept telling me I should be pitching furiously for work and making stuff happen and reorganizing the basement instead of waiting for cosmic intervention seemed determined to take up all my headspace.

Tuning in to our inner voice should be easy, right? People say 'just listen to your gut' or 'trust your instincts', but that can be difficult when your gut is on high alert for impending doom. I've spent years fighting off gut feelings that were all about what could go wrong. Cars that could crash, gas hobs I could have left on, babies who could die if I didn't check on them every 15 minutes, day and night (true story).

My mind has no trouble imagining worst-case scenarios and making them seem as if they need my urgent attention. And this occasion was no exception. I was outside my comfort zone and the voice in my head that likes to sound an alarm every few minutes was really going for it. *What if you never work again? What if you never find the right thing? Who do you think you are, taking time out to just see what happens? Who are you to think you deserve something better? When are you ever going to earn any money?*

I decided there was no time to waste. If my inner voice had helped me to know my worth and quit while I was ahead with my magazine job, could it come up with the goods now and help me work out what to do next? I needed to get in touch with it, and fast. So I descended upon the internet in search of experts and advice and magical shortcuts. I was drowning in articles, theories and meditation methods when my friend Fiona – of post-funeral Diet Coke and crisps fame – came to my rescue.

She became a life coach years before the discipline exploded onto social media and into the public consciousness. 'This is such a common problem for my clients,' she told me. 'You'd be amazed by how many people have exactly the same issue with tuning in to their intuition when life gets stressful. Even the ones who look like they've got it all together are quietly experiencing massive internal conflict!'

Fiona explained that the difference between the voice of anxiety and the voice of intuition is that anxiety is based on fear whereas intuition comes from somewhere calm. If I could locate that calm place, and tune in to the right voice, I'd be good to go.

'You have a decision to make and you want your intuition to lead the way instead of your inner critic,' she said. 'The easiest way to achieve that is to get out of your head and into your body. If you learn to observe both your anxious, critical voice and your intuitive voice without judgement, and tune in to how they make you feel, you'll be able to tell which is which – and work out which of the options you're deciding between feels most right for you.'

Fiona suggested I think back to a time when I was sure my intuitive voice had been talking and another when I knew it had been anxiety or fear. I thought about the way I always feel when I read tarot cards and how I'd felt after that new-moon meditation back in April. She was right – this latest onslaught of anxious questioning had made me forget that I actually *do* know when my intuition is talking. And it really does come from a calm place.

Thinking about my anxious voice was much more uncomfortable. I considered all the times I'd filed magazine features absolutely convinced that I'd made some heinous spelling or factual error that would end in disaster. I thought about the voice that had taken over after my daughter Lola was born, constantly telling me I was getting everything and anything wrong.

I thought about the voice I kept hearing now, on repeat – the one that was squeezing the joy out of everything with its incessant chatter. Deep down, I guess I knew that the voice that was shouting the loudest was the one coming from a place of fear.

Fiona suggested I give these two voices their own characters, to make them even more distinct in my mind and give me a better chance of taking control of them. She asked me lots of questions to uncover the voices' characteristics. I decided that my intuitive voice was a magical talking moon. And my anxious, fear-driven one? I thought back to The Goblin oracle card at that Bristol yoga class years earlier and decided to give him the role!

Next, she taught me a body scan meditation I could use to really tune in to how the two different options I currently had on the table (basically, continue going with the flow or start pitching features again right this second) made me feel, without the intrusive thought-reel getting in the way. After talking me through some breathing techniques to help me get in the zone, Fiona asked me to imagine myself in the latter scenario.

I visualized it all in detail. The emails. The pitches. The deadlines. The hustle. The thrill of picking up a magazine in the supermarket and flicking through it to find my work. I pictured the invoices. I felt the stress. I heard the tap-tap-tap of my manic typing. I heard myself shouting 'one more minute' to my children as I pressed send on an email. I imagined the taste of the cold cup of tea I'd sip before realizing it was several hours old.

Then she asked me to 'scan' my body from head to toe, noticing but not judging how that visualization made me feel. It wasn't good! Even just imagining being back on that treadmill made me feel tense, tight and as if I couldn't breathe properly. My body knew it wasn't right for me to listen to The Goblin.

I went back in to visualize the other option – the one I'd been happily enjoying until my thoughts went haywire. Without as much real-life experience to draw on, it was harder to picture, but I let my imagination roll. I visualized myself as I was in the here and now, living life in the slow lane for the first time in years. I visualized myself writing more posts for my Mystical Thinking blog. I imagined people actually reading them. I saw myself diving deeper into the mystical world.

I indulged in a vision of myself in a perfect crow pose, mastered while wearing Lululemon yoga pants. And I threw in another vision of my bank balance with a glaring red minus for realism. But then I imagined the sound of my children laughing as they kicked up autumn leaves in the park. And I breathed in the smell of banana bread fresh from the oven. I saw myself relaxed and happy, wearing stain-free cashmere and living in the moment.

Hold on a minute, wasn't this just a fantasy? It certainly felt like one. I forced myself back to the bank balance part of my vision. It might be considered spiritual to eschew capitalism and materialism and consumer culture but I still had bills to pay and kids who needed school shoes. I couldn't visualize my way out of that, no matter how hard I tried. And I was burning through my overdraft. I also imagined myself having nothing to say when someone asked me what my job was. Who am I without my job in journalism? Isn't that what makes me interesting? Isn't that who I am?

When I tried the body scan meditation for the 'fantasy' option, I was surprised by the results. My mind might have been conflicted but the rest of me felt good. Really good. It felt right. I felt calm and relaxed, grounded even. My body didn't seem to care about my net worth or having nothing impressive to show off about at parties. I could feel my magical talking moon shining down upon me.

'It's all about giving yourself new information to work with,' Fiona explained after I'd described what I'd felt. 'It's difficult to make rational decisions when fear takes over, but the energy you feel in your body doesn't lie.'

The experience was enough to convince me to stick it out in my strangely slow new world just a little bit longer. My Goblin was still running riot at times, but I soon found I could listen to him in a detached way and know it was my anxious voice talking. And the more I practised the body scan meditation, the more I tuned in to the feeling that told me when a choice was right for me. I began to feel that I was in tune with my intuition. I began to notice the difference between The Goblin and the magical talking moon and pay attention to the latter.

And just like that, day by day, practice made perfect. I soon started to realize that my intuition was always right. And that it'd been right there all along. The voice that told me a friend's motives weren't quite what they seemed, and that backing away was a better choice than bending myself to fit in, proved shockingly correct when I found myself watching lives I cared about implode from a distance. The hunch I'd had back in May that my work for the magazine was going nowhere fast became an email announcing that the company was now in administration. The quiet voice back in April that had told me to just keep going when I meditated with the moon was repeating the same thing now, every time I tuned in. The certain knowledge that some of the people I connected with were meant for me and me for them became a loud and clear yes every time.

> *The more I tuned in to my intuition, the more I realized it knew what was what.*

The more I tuned in to my inner voice with meditation and journalling, the more confidence I had in it. The more I trusted myself, the easier it was to make decisions. And the more I surprised myself with the kind of thinking I would previously have dismissed in a heartbeat.

Towards the end of September one particular meditation and journalling session ended in the kind of revelation I know I would once have ignored. I was doing some freewriting (letting the pen move across the paper without thinking or judging and just seeing what came out) when I saw myself scrawl the words 'You don't have to just be a writer,' across the page.

It felt as if my heart had stopped beating for a second. Writing was my life. What could this possibly mean? But then I tuned in to how calm I felt and I knew it was a message from my magical talking moon, my intuition.

It was time to make some big decisions, new decisions, decisions that would take me way out of my comfort zone. And when I say that decisions have long been the bane of my life, I'm really not exaggerating. Small and inconsequential (drinks, snacks, near-identical pairs of shoes) or potentially life-changing (house moves, job moves, school admission forms), for much of my life if there was a decision to be made you could guarantee I'd overthink it until the eleventh hour before possibly failing to make it at all.

In the time I've spent agonizing, overanalysing and researching potential holiday destinations to world-expert level (if you ever want to know where to stay in Tulum, Mexico, I've one hell of a spreadsheet) I probably could have found the answer to world peace or written a novel, or at least not given myself palpitations over the fact that all beach huts are not created equal.

For years I passed off my indecisiveness as a quirk, an inevitable part of my Piscean sun sign personality, along with daydreaming and flakiness and idealistic visions. I also tried to claim that my tendency to research the hell out of everything was part and parcel of my decades-long journalism career.

I even tried to convince myself that it was kind of cute. Ah, poor Emma, she can't make a decision to save her life – someone order from the breakfast menu for her and put her out of her misery! But it wasn't cute. It was time-consuming, painful and incredibly irritating for the people around me.

Even when I did make a decision, I'd find myself doubting it and wondering about it and trying to go back on it before I finally committed. Sometimes I found that I'd spent more time trying to *make* a decision than I needed to spend *doing* the thing I was deciding about. It was tedious and exhausting. And it filled up my laptop with documents packed with flight times and school catchment distances and screenshots of identical Mexican smoothie bowls. We never even took that trip to Tulum.

I'd never really paid much attention to *why* I found decision-making so agonizing or why I'd spent so much of my life avoiding it, until I realized that my mystical year was beginning to change my approach. And learning to tune in to my intuition and my inner voice was a big part of it. I was slowly becoming someone who actually *could* decide.

It was an unexpected side effect of my mystical year, and yet possibly the most life-changing development of all. Whether I was believing in rainbow signs, feeling my way to the answers, or just not doing a massive eye-roll every time someone suggested I let my intuition guide me to the right choice, slowly but surely my struggle with indecision was becoming a thing of the past.

But if I wasn't only to be a writer, what was I going to be? My inner voice had posed a question I realized I wanted to answer. I'd been mulling over the idea of learning reiki for months: I liked the idea of engaging in a practice that wasn't about analysing or thinking, something that was more about doing.

> *I liked the idea of learning something new; something I didn't fully understand; something I might never understand.*

I liked the idea of stepping out from behind my computer screen, making connections in the real world and maybe even helping other people in the process. I decided it was time to stop mulling it over and start looking for a reiki teacher. And with intuition on my side, what would once have taken me hours of overthinking, an Excel spreadsheet and 14 different conversations with friends, asking for opinions, was nailed in minutes.

I began by looking for reiki teachers who were local to my home in Kent, but something (my inner voice) told me to try looking in East Sussex instead (I live on the border of the two counties). And there she was – right at the top of my Google search, as if she'd been waiting for me all along. I knew that Jackie from St Leonard's Reiki was the right teacher for me the moment I clicked on her website. I could feel it.

She had time in her schedule and was willing to teach me one-on-one in a day. We were both free on the same convenient date in November. It was all so simple it felt a bit ridiculous. And I couldn't believe how quickly I had it all organized. I put it in my diary, sent Jackie a deposit and didn't give it another thought. It was liberating.

Once I got into using my intuition to make decisions like this there was no stopping me. I could decide anything simply by tuning in to how it made me feel and listening to the right voice. Motorway route or country back roads? Take the job or keep looking? Book the flight or wait and see if it gets cheaper? I soon began to realize that actually making *any* decision was better than *not* making one. I started making them all the time. As if it was nothing.

It felt as if my mystical year was finally beginning to put me back together again.

Do it yourself – tune in to your intuition

If you've never struggled to make a decision in your life then what I've just described may sound like a bit of a non-event. But if you have, I know you'll get it. And even if you eat decisions for breakfast, there's magic to be found in really tuning in to your intuition.

For me, it was empowering. I could tune in to my inner world and actually trust what I found there. And realizing that life doesn't have to be complicated or angst-ridden or overloaded by endless doubt was the light-bulb moment I'd been waiting for.

Life could be easy and flowing and peaceful and calm. All I had to do was look within. And maybe that means you could do the same, because your inner wisdom, your inner knowing, your intuition really is the GPS of your soul. And once you've got that on your side, everything becomes a little bit easier. Here are a few ways to tell the difference between intuition and your inner critic.

Intuition	Inner critic
Feels peaceful	Feels like fear
No difficult physical feelings	Fast heartbeat or breathing
Gives you a relaxed, positive feeling	Gives you a panicky, stressed-out feeling
A calm message that says what it has to and then leaves	A repetitive, demanding voice in your head that won't leave you alone
Feels right or good in the body	Feels uncomfortable or tense in the body

October

MAGICAL PLACES & MANIFESTATION

Celebration: Samhain (Halloween)	
Moon: Hunter's moon	
Sign: Libra	
Crystal: Opal	
Element: Air	
Tarot: Justice	

Just say yes

> 'So, you're basically going to
> Australia for the weekend?'
>
> SCHOOL-GATE MUM

I knew how it looked. I knew it was ridiculous. I knew I'd be paying off the credit card bill for years. But there's nothing quite like boarding a plane at London Heathrow on a chilly October evening and arriving in Sydney for a spring sunrise to make a girl believe in magic.

I never cancelled the flight to Australia I'd booked on a whim back in May. Better than that, I'd actually RSVP'd yes to the bride-to-be and booked five nights in an Airbnb in Byron Bay.

When the time came, I dropped my girls off at their grandmother's for the week and asked my husband to pick them up when he finished work the following Friday. I packed the lightest of solo travel bags, flinging in sandals and summer dresses and matching nail varnish with the wild abandon of someone who's never had to navigate airport security with a toddler in tow. I ordered sleeping pills from a corner of the internet I'd never visited before. But most importantly… I got on the plane.

You don't have to say it – I *know!* I was tempted to leave this particular mystical adventure out of this story, for obvious reasons. Talk about a contradiction! I'd deliberately set out to make my life feel magical again *without* buying plane tickets to far-flung places or spending money I didn't have on a fast track to inner peace.

But to skip this part would mean bypassing the truth. And the truth was that this trip – whether I'd manifested it by miracle, magic, or the plain old privilege of owning a credit card and having a relative willing to look after my children – began with a desire to see my friend Jane walk down the aisle but ended up becoming something much bigger. This trip was the ultimate *yes* – a high-five to freedom. And I hope it might also be an ever-so-slightly crazy example of what can happen if you too allow yourself to believe in magic.

When I'd made my vision board back in January, I'd plastered it with pictures of beaches and sunsets and open roads but I had no real idea of where the year would take me. I knew I'd spend the summer in Skiathos, but I didn't know that Jane had even picked a date for her wedding.

And I'm pretty sure that when she sent me an invitation, it was in the almost certain knowledge that I'd have to decline. Because that was the obvious response; that was the sensible answer; that was the 'I'm a mother and I have responsibilities and you live 10,000 miles away' answer. If I'd received that wedding invitation any other year, I'm quite sure I would have said a polite no. And I'm putting my yes down to the power of manifestation.

Vision boards, journalling, affirmations, writing yourself multimillion-dollar cheques (as once practised by a broke and jobless Jim Carrey), manifestation has fast become the self-help trend it's impossible to avoid.

And it's not just Carrey – everyone's at it. Oprah is a long-term fan, crediting her role in the 1985 film *The Color Purple* with her belief in the power of the universe, while British writer Bernardine Evaristo visualized herself winning the Booker Prize many years before it became a reality. The mantras of fame that Stefani Germanotta once repeated over and over came magically true when she became Lady Gaga. And for singer Lizzo, the words 'coconut oil' written on a list of New Year's resolutions turned into an album of the same name.

It's not just celebrities, either – it's Instagram influencers, it's mums on the school run, it was me, right at the beginning of this book, when I made myself that 2018 vision board and wondered if it would deliver. Have you made a vision board? Has yours started to deliver?

It's easy to see why the concept of manifestation holds so much appeal for so many people. Thinking your way to love, money and a better reality is the kind of mystical action anyone would want a piece of. The premise is simple enough – if you can dream it, you can do it; if you can believe it, you can receive it; if you vibrate at a high level, those vibrations will materialize into your heart's desire. Hang on a minute while I just think myself up a personal assistant, five more hours in the day and a return to the lightning-fast metabolism of my 19-year-old self.

Manifestation is, of course, not quite that simple. It requires an element of positive action, for starters – change, work, bravery, planning, speaking up, standing firm. That Academy Award didn't just land in Lady Gaga's lap, you know!

Manifestation isn't without its issues, either. There's no escaping the disconnect that occurs when you turn the Law of Attraction on its head. If someone's life is difficult or challenging or fraught with sadness and pain, are we really expected to believe it's because they don't think positively enough? Or that their vibration never gets high enough for the universe to throw them a line?

As much as I love the idea of thoughts becoming realities and dreams coming true, I don't buy that for a second. We're not all starting from the same point here. Manifesting your dream life and a wardrobe full of Louboutins – or, let's face it, a plane ticket to the other side of the world – is a hell of a lot easier when you're starting from a place of privilege.

The principles of manifestation may not be perfect but that doesn't mean they're without value. I'm pretty sure that anyone can benefit from sprinkling a bit of fairy dust on the concept of goal setting. After all, when was the last time you got heart-stoppingly, can't-catch-your-breath excited about a sensible five-year plan? Building up savings, climbing the ladder, finally getting round to sorting out that will? No, not really doing it for me!

> *Manifestation allows us to dream. It allows us to imagine the unimaginable.*

It gives us permission to think beyond other people's expectations and the boxes we put ourselves in. It dares us to imagine the life we might create for ourselves if there were no limits. And then it challenges us to believe that's already the case. It asks us what we'd do if we could do anything. And as far as that part is concerned, I'm all in.

That January vision board kick-started something for me – something that switched up my mindset and became a real-world manifestation of a cut-and-paste picture. I began to see solutions where I would once have seen problems. I began to allow myself to dream big. I began to see magic and joy and potential in places where I would once have seen unnecessary indulgence that I didn't deserve. I became the kind of person who gets on the plane. And I'm so glad I did.

If I hadn't got on that plane, I wouldn't have seen the magical golden glow of that Sydney sunrise. Nor would I have devoured a massive Lebanese mezze plate for breakfast as I waited in domestic departures for my internal flight connection (and, honestly, that houmous was worth the trip in itself). I wouldn't have dropped off my bags at a not-quite-ready Airbnb, grabbed a towel and taken a jet-lagged stroll to the beach.

I wouldn't have gazed, transfixed, at those big-sky views and Byron Bay's enormous stretch of pale yellow sand. If I hadn't got on that plane, I wouldn't have walked into the cool crashing waves of the Pacific Ocean and immersed myself from head to toe. And I wouldn't have sat watching dreamers and drifters and barefoot children gather in a circle to drum down the sunset, their silhouettes dancing against a fading sorbet sky. I really am glad I got on that plane.

A laidback beach town on the east coast of Australia, Byron Bay has the kind of counterculture hippie vibe I was always going to fall in love with. And that's exactly what happened when I first found myself there as a wide-eyed backpacker in a different millennium. I remember an old guy on the beach – he was probably all of 30! – who told me a story about the ley lines and the obsidian-threaded bedrock beneath the land on which the town was built, and being quite sure I could feel the mystical energy.

Look out across a seascape sunrise from the Cape Bryon Lighthouse (the most easterly point in Australia) and you feel as though you're on the edge of the Earth. If there's a more perfect setting for a long weekend of friends and fun and love and magic than Byron Bay, I don't know where it is.

'This is like a miracle or something! I just can't believe you're actually here!' exclaimed my childhood friend Annie, fresh off the evening flight from Melbourne.

'I know!' I replied. 'Imagine if we could go back in time to 90s Yorkshire and tell our 14-year-old selves we'd be meeting up here for Jane's wedding in 2018!'

'We'd never have believed it!' Annie said.

My grown-up self could hardly believe it, either. We knew we didn't have long together so we packed it all in. We set the world to rights under starry skies. We got up at dawn to post smug pictures of green smoothies and beach yoga on Instagram. We ate Tim Tam biscuits and avocado brunches and browsed fairy-light-lit night markets full of crystals and tie-dye T-shirts and homemade hemp soap.

We took a trip down backpacker memory lane to inhale the second-hand marijuana smoke of languid 20-somethings stretched out in the sun at hostels we'd stayed in years earlier. We walked and we talked and we tried on the kind of expensive bohemian dresses we'd need more of, just as soon as we worked out a way to make this our life for the rest of forever. We got manicures to match our wedding outfits.

We slipped down a side street to an alternative health centre called the Byron Bay Medicine Wheel for reiki treatments and psychic sessions and tarot readings that sent shivers down my spine.

'There's a man here,' said the tarot reader as she laid cards out before me. 'He's called John, or maybe Patrick… does that mean anything to you?'

'Those are my late father-in-law's names,' I said.

'He thinks you should keep going with the project you started, if that makes any sense?' she continued.

'It doesn't and it does at the same time,' I replied, my mind blown. I wasn't that surprised to receive a message from beyond the veil, but John seemed the most unlikely choice of mystical messenger.

Less than 48 hours had passed when Annie and I met up with the bride-to-be for a pre-wedding last-hurrah dinner, and yet I felt as if I'd been on a month-long retreat. The three of us dived into goose-bumps nostalgia without pausing for breath or ordering anything like enough main courses. Coupé cocktails, shoestring fries, school days and in-jokes, magic and misery, hazy hometown memories cast in a golden light through the rear-view mirror. I love it when shared history means you don't have to explain who you are. When you can pick up a conversation you left off a decade earlier.

I hadn't thought about my inner child since my July crystal reading but I felt as if I was in touch with her now. She was running through a gap in the heather on Ilkley Moor. She was scraping names into metal pencil cases with the sharp end of a compass. She was dancing on a picnic bench in a pub garden after dark.

And she was here in Australia, with friends who knew everything about her and loved her all the same. Friends who'll forever remember her as she was back then. We all needed that night to remind us who we once were and who we might yet become. Turns out that ditching the UK for dreamy Australian beaches the first chance you get doesn't make a person immune to the pressures of life in the modern world.

When I watched Jane walk down a tropical garden aisle in a wisp of lace a few days later, I got everything I'd come for. She was smiling and radiant beneath a floral arch, her two daughters by her side. She was laughing at speeches next to the love of her life. She was dancing to a-ha in the dark, perilously close to the edge of a blue-lit pool. Once again, I was glad I'd got on that plane.

Annie and I spent our last day together a few miles out of town, in a wooden cabin in the middle of a tea tree forest. It was a take-it-to-the-wire panic booking in a place we thought was a last resort because everywhere else was full. We couldn't have been more wrong. It was so magical I was sure one of those ley lines must be involved.

I etched our final stroll along the vast expanse of beach at Lennox Head (a village known for its amazing surf breaks) into my memory before it had even finished, along with the cool, dark swim we took in a mystical tea tree lake. That night we lit a fire outside the cabin under a Taurus full moon (my moon sign) and watched as the wood began to crackle and spark. And then we wrote down everything we wanted to let go of or release from our lives and burnt the lists to ash – the perfect ceremony to mark 10 mystical months and two more left to go.

The year so far had cast the best kind of spell on me. I'd blown caution to the wind for the first time in years. When life gets bogged down with grown-up responsibilities and people who rely on you, finding a way to feel free can be a challenge. Life moves on, worlds change, youthful free spirits become people with jobs and car insurance and debt consolidation loans to repay. But does that really mean we can no longer turn a no into a yes? Especially if it's a yes we really want?

I might have felt ridiculous explaining to that mum at the school gates that I really was flying across the world for a long weekend, but I didn't regret making it happen. Byron Bay is a magical place and it was exactly what I needed. But you really don't need to travel 10,000 miles to find that kind of magic.

There are magical places all over the world, and closer to home, if you choose to seek them out.

If it's hippie vibes and eco living in the UK you're after, take a trip to Glastonbury, Totnes, Stroud, Brighton or Hebden Bridge. If you want crystal-threaded bedrock beneath your feet, you'll find fluorite in Derbyshire and amber resin in Suffolk and garnet in Ruby Bay in Fife, Scotland. If your heart beats faster at the thought of a stone circle, it won't take long to find one in Yorkshire or Wiltshire or Dartmoor in Devon.

That's not the half of it, either. There's more than enough magic to go round. Try the Mermaid's Pool in the Peak District, or Giant's Causeway in Northern Ireland. Or how about the wilds of the California desert, or sunset in Deià, Mallorca, or the pyramids in Egypt, or the birthplace of yoga, Rishikesh in India? Or try your own back garden at the break of dawn, or a flowing stream at the bottom of a field, or a wild wood carpeted with bluebells – or absolutely anywhere you can think of with some grass and a few trees.

Roald Dahl once said that 'Those who don't believe in magic will never find it,' and I really think he was right. Perhaps we could all benefit from allowing a little more of it to seep into our souls.

'I'm so glad you made the trip over here,' said Annie in a text a few weeks later. 'I feel like my whole outlook on life has changed! I've booked a course of yoga classes! I'm embracing early mornings! I've applied for a new job!'

'That'll be the Byron Bay magic,' I replied.

'Or maybe it was our magic,' she typed back.

'Our magic,' I repeated. 'I like the sound of that.'

Do it yourself – manifest your dreams

I'm not going to suggest that you book a seat on the next flight to Australia, but I am going to suggest that you ask yourself if there's something that you'd like to say yes to. Something that you want to manifest into reality. Something that makes your heart beat faster in all the right ways.

Why can't you make that weekend away with your friends happen? Who says you can't do the course you've been dreaming about? Why shouldn't you take a break? What would happen if you put yourself first? What might life become if you went for your big dream? What if you let yourself live more?

What would you do if the world really was your oyster? What if you quit the job you hate? What if you really could spend more time doing what you love? What if you just did the thing or took the trip or made the break or let it go? What if you allowed yourself to become the person you want to be?

Here's how to make a dream come true:

Get a goal

First, you need to decide exactly what it is that you really want – love, friendship, money, a new career or something else. Allow yourself to think outside the box: this isn't about five-year plans or ticking off life goals you're not even sure you care about. If you're struggling to tune in to what you really want out of life, try meditating, making an intuitive vision board (see the January chapter), or journalling about it (my favourite journalling exercise, 'In my best life I wake up and...', as featured in the March chapter, is great for a surprise revelation or two).

Imagine it fully

Once you've got your answer, it's time for the fun part – visualizing it. Imagine your goal being realized in as much detail as possible, using whatever method works best for you. That might be as straightforward as closing your eyes and fully imagining yourself in your dream home surrounded by people you love. Or it might mean writing at length about your perfect job – describing everything from the outfit you wear on your first day to how you feel as you sit in that corner office with your name on the door.

Or it might mean creating a virtual or physical visual representation of the future you want to create for yourself. Just make sure you cover every aspect of it so it feels as real as possible. Engage all of your senses. Allow yourself to feel the way you'd feel if your heart's desire really did become a reality.

Let go

If you want to invite something new and magical into your life you might need to make some space. Get really honest with yourself about the limiting beliefs, old ways of thinking or unhealthy habits that are holding you back... and then let them go. See the April chapter for tips on using the power of the moon to do this.

Do the work

Remember what I said earlier about Lady Gaga and her Academy Award? It applies to you too, unfortunately. If your big dream is to write a book, you won't get very far if you never put pen to paper (trust me, I tried to do it that way for years!) If you're looking for someone to share your life with, you won't find them if you refuse to make a single new connection. Be honest with yourself about the small steps you can take to show the universe how much you mean it!

Keep believing

Basically, stay as positive as humanly possible. I know that isn't always the easiest task, so use all the tricks you can, whenever you need to. Try writing a gratitude list or repeating affirmations. Keep up those visualizations. Notice the small things that make you happy. Talk to yourself as though you already have the thing you want the most. Do what you love whenever you can. Know that your moment is coming like you know your own name.

Be open to something even better

I'm not sure where I first read about this trick, but whenever I write a manifestation missive I always sign off with the words 'This or something better', to let the universe know it can up its game if it fancies. And you know what, often it does.

November

DIY MAGIC & SPIRITUAL ACTIVISM

Celebration: World Kindness Day

Moon: Beaver moon

Sign: Scorpio

Crystal: Citrine

Element: Water

Tarot: Death

Totally that witch

'Light as a feather. stiff as a board.'

SLEEPOVER 'LEVITATION' GAME

There's nothing remotely magical about clearing up the detritus left after a children's Halloween party when you're so jet-lagged you want to weep, but that's where I found myself as November began. I took down spooky decorations, scrubbed trodden-in mud off the kitchen floor and did my best to reunite lost wands and pointy witch hats with their rightful junior owners.

It certainly felt like the season of the witch. Witches were everywhere. They were in millennial trend features in glossy magazines and in copy-cat tabloid clickbait; they were on Netflix in a new adaptation of 90s classic *Sabrina the Teenage Witch*; they were posting stylish flat-lays (bird's-eye-view photographs) of tarot cards and pentagrams all over social media with the hashtag *#witchesofinstagram*.

And when I opened *The Sunday Times Style* magazine to read my horoscope on a quiet November weekend, there was one there too: Amanda Yates Garcia, the Oracle of LA, a working witch with an A-list clientele who had become known for putting a hex on Donald Trump. I was here for it. It felt as if the whole world was starting to believe in magic.

 I've always believed in magic. And if you've ever made a wish on a birthday-cake candle or a shooting star, in a way, you have too.

Much of my Yorkshire childhood was spent grinding up flower petals to make magical perfume or stirring leafy potions with an old twig at the bottom of the garden. By the time I reached my teenage witch years, I was something of a magic pro. And absolutely certain I could make things happen with my ad hoc spells.

Of course, at the time, that mostly meant love spells. And lots of them. And 'please let me do well in the biology test' spells. And 'please make my parents say that I can go to the party at the weekend' spells.

There was never a shortage of wishes over which to wave a wand for myself and my friends. I used candles and sigils (a sort of magical monogram; more on these later) and invocations I pretty much made up on the spot. I was absolutely certain they worked. I cast a spell to help a friend get a slow dance to Robin Beck's 'First Time' at the school disco with a boy she liked – and watched as the awkward shuffle she'd dreamt of became a reality in the gym. I cast a spell to make my favourite topic come up in my A-level psychology exam – and it appeared right at the top of the page. I cast spells for love and spells for luck and spells to try and speed up time so I could grow up and step out into a world that was bigger and more exciting than the one I lived in.

Years later, when the magic of time had made that last one come true, I cast spells for jobs and money and perfect flats. In 2002, when my friends and I wanted to find a place we could afford near the Tube and a decent pub – a pretty big ask in North London at the time – I lit the biggest green candle I could find for luck. And after weeks of false starts and dodgy-sounding landlords, that candle magic led us to the perfect location the very next day, minutes from the Tube and a pub with a leafy beer garden.

Once, I even tried a binding spell, like the hex that Amanda Yates Garcia had put on Donald Trump – although mine wasn't for quite such a worthy reason. I'd had my heart broken by a boy in a band whose romantic declarations dissolved into cliché the minute the chase was over. 'This isn't going to work out after all,' he said, the moment I woke up beside him.

I never wanted to see him again but he'd just signed a record deal and I began to live in fear of his face taunting me from advertising billboards forever. I felt wronged and self-righteous and ready for revenge. So I carved a sigil into a candle in my flat and watched it burn down, willing him to never make it so big that I'd have to hear his voice on the radio.

To be fair to the ghosts of romances past, I was being a bit dramatic, and that boy actually went on to have an incredibly successful career. When I saw him at a mutual friend's wedding in 2014, he was blissfully happy, about to go on tour with his band and newly engaged to a very famous *Friends* star. He was no longer a frontman, though. And you know what, I've never heard his voice on the radio. Just putting that out there. Maybe magic *does* work!

By 2018, I no longer had any dubious love interests to banish for all eternity, but whenever push came to shove on something that mattered to me, I still liked to turn to a spell. At the start of November, I found myself carving a sigil based on the word 'magic' into a candle, to try and keep the Byron Bay vibes alive and kicking for as long as I could.

And, of course, even when I wasn't consciously creating spells, I was making magic. Those everyday rituals I'd incorporated into my life in March. *Magic*. The moon rituals that had become part of the ebb and flow of my months. *Magic*. The tarot cards, the spirit guides, the midnight star-gazing. *Magic. Magic. Magic.* And also, I realized to my horror, all pretty *Me. Me. Me.*

The idea of hexing heinous presidents and using spells to make the world a better place had got me thinking. In the wake of the #MeToo movement, it felt like the world was changing. Women were marching in their millions. Harvey Weinstein had been arrested. Bill Cosby had been sentenced. Professor Christine Blasey Ford had stood up to testify against Supreme Court nominee Brett Kavanaugh.

An image of a woman holding a banner saying 'We are the granddaughters of the witches you weren't able to burn' was doing the rounds on social media. Identifying as a witch no longer felt like something to hide. I wasn't sure I'd be dropping it into the school-gate chat just yet, but still, I felt the shift.

> *Witchcraft was power. Witchcraft was activism. Witchcraft was standing up to be counted on things that matter.*

It felt as if the time of the Goddess had come. And time that I found a way to make a difference. Even I was a bit sick of my own navel-gazing by now.

I started by switching up my spell work. I made a vision board for a better world and carved a peace sign into a white candle. I sent good vibes to friends facing heartbreak and health challenges and pulled oracle cards for stressed-out strangers online. Much of my mystical year so far had been about looking within in my quest for inner peace, and it was working: I felt better than I had done in years. I'd seen for myself what can happen if you tune in, slow down and open up to the powers of the universe. Turning some of that attention outwards was the obvious next step.

There was no shortage of external issues for me to focus on, either. Britain was a Brexit-induced mess of division, inequality and racism. California was burning. Children were being separated from their parents at the US/Mexico border. The world was as cruel and divisive and unfair as it had ever been. And I wasn't sure that a sigil on a candle was really going to cut it.

Inner peace might be an inside job but making the world a better place definitely isn't. I'd felt the disconnect between the love-and-light posts I scrolled past on social media and what I saw on the news. I knew that the challenges and complexities of human experience couldn't all be fixed with positive vibes. I knew that posting spiritual memes on the internet wasn't going to change anything.

I also knew I had it easy. I began to wonder if I'd spent so much time worrying about my own issues in 2018 that I'd put myself in a mystical vacuum. There would always be room in my life for inspirational quotes and magic spells, but I didn't want to go another day without turning magic into *action*. It was time I made my mystical year about more than just me.

I started small. I did what I could. I put what money I had where my mouth was. I found a legal fund that had been set up to help those separated children at the US/Mexico border and made a donation. I reinstated a Greenpeace membership I'd let lapse a while back. I talked to my children about Extinction Rebellion and climate change and what mattered most to them when it came to their own futures.

We joined the WWF and sponsored a polar bear. I stopped skipping over Facebook food bank appeals because I had too much work on and couldn't be bothered to find my credit card right that second. I started actively trying to find ways I could make a difference to the world outside my window. And I started thinking about what else I could do to make the world a better place. It felt like a step in the right direction.

There is, of course, nothing wrong with focusing in on yourself and getting your own house in order, mentally, physically and spiritually. In fact, this might just be one of the most important things any of us will ever do. It's difficult to focus on the world around you when you're falling apart, but once you start feeling good again paying it forward can create the most magical ripple effect.

I was no longer in the burnt-out and broken place I'd found myself at the start of the year. I was ready for something more. And it felt as if the rest of the world might be ready too. Those glossy mag Insta-witches were just the start of it. I began to notice a shift in the way people around me engaged with the mystical world. And I'm at least 80 per cent certain they weren't just being polite.

Fellow mums on the school run started to ask me questions about moon rituals. My friends' children wanted to talk about their crystal collections. Everyone around me seemed to be signing up for yoga classes or talking about journalling and meditation. I was nearly at the end of my mystical year and I suddenly had more volunteers ready and willing to join me on my mystical adventures than ever before.

It was a shift that planted a seed in my mind, the very beginnings of a plan. I wondered if I could share the mystical world with those around me in a way that went beyond clicking 'publish' on blog and Instagram posts. I wondered if I could find a way to bring people together in the real world to share their own stories, make connections and feel part of something bigger. Could I find a way to make life feel magical again for other people as well as myself?

If I could combine that with enough magical action, perhaps I'd have found my purpose. I also wondered if I should just get on with it and join that hex on Donald Trump. My mystical year was changing and evolving and becoming something new. It was no longer just about me.

Do it yourself – make your own kind of magic

If you're interested in witchcraft or spellwork there are all sorts of ways you can begin to make your own magic. Here are five suggestions for easy ways to power up your wishes, goals and intentions and make life feel magical again. See also the March chapter for candle and colour magic.

Create a sigil

Sigils are powerful symbols used to represent magical intentions. To create one all you need to do is write down what you're aiming for (inner peace, for example) and then cross out all the vowels and any repeated letters in the words (in this case you'd end up with the letters n, r, p and c). You then play around, joining the letters together and moving them about until you create a magical symbol out of them; the less it resembles the original word the better.

This symbol, or sigil, can then be carved into a candle, drawn on something for luck (clothes labels is a good one), or written down and burnt into the ether to help make your wish come true.

Power up your altar

I talked about altars – a special space in your house where you can spend time tuning in, display magical items and make magic – in the March chapter, but they definitely deserve another mention here.

Think of your altar as the power centre of your mystical practice – a sort of magical HQ for casting spells and contemplating intentions. Switch it up regularly, adding items chosen to represent whatever you're trying to welcome into your life (for example, tarot cards, crystals, ancestor offerings, inspiring images, candles carved with sigils, or items that represent the four elements or directions).

Make moon water

Making your own super-charged lunar water is an easy way to tune in to the magic of the moon. Leave a glass or a jug of water outside (or on a window sill) on the full moon (check out which astrological sign the moon is in for more magical insights) and use it to power up your intentions, add a boost to a ritual bath or cleanse your crystals. You can even drink it if you like!

Herbal magic

If you fancy delving deeper into the world of magic using herbs, essential oils and crystals, I recommend Semra Haksever's book

Everyday Magic. It's easy to follow and packed with spells for manifestation, courage, love and everything in between.

Take action

Choose a cause you believe in and pledge to take positive action to support it. This doesn't have to mean financial support, if you're not in a position to do that right now – action can also take the form of campaigning, petitioning, protesting, sharing social media posts and taking a stand when it matters most. Educate your children. Learn from them. Take care of the world around you. And call out hatred and prejudice whenever you see it.

Becoming my own healer

> 'You have the power to heal your life.'
> LOUISE HAY

'Just for today, I will not worry,' said Jackie as she showed me how to place one of my hands at my root chakra and the other at my heart. I'd taken the train to the East Sussex coast to learn reiki and she was talking me through its five ethical principles.

'Just for today, I will not be angry,' she continued as I switched my heart hand to my third eye (otherwise known as my forehead).

'Just for today, I will do my work honestly. Just for today, I will give thanks for my many blessings. Just for today, I will be kind to my neighbour and every living thing.'

I let out a long exhale. There wasn't much to argue with here: living in the moment with gratitude and kindness, and waving goodbye to worry, anger and deceit, sounded like a pretty good blueprint for life. I was glad I'd made the decision to add the energy healing therapy reiki to my mystical toolkit, and we'd barely even begun.

Reiki is the Japanese word for universal life-force energy. 'Rei' means universal (a mysterious essence, spirit, soul or higher power) and 'ki' means life force or vital energy, which is similar in meaning to the Sanskrit term *prana* I'd learnt years earlier in yoga. It's believed that universal life-force energy is present in all living things.

Learning about reiki and receiving an 'attunement' (which is what I was hanging out on the coast for) helps to open up a channel for this life-force energy, enabling it to flow freely. Think of it as an initiation: the life-force energy may already be present but the attunement ritual – which passes reiki from master to student – helps power up the intention to channel it. The channelling of this energy is said to accelerate the body's ability to heal itself (note: this isn't the same as curing itself), reduce stress and promote wellbeing. Best of all, reiki is a therapy you can use to treat yourself.

I'd tried out a few different energy practitioners and treatments since my session in the shed with Myra in July, and I'd got a lot out of all of them, but I really liked the idea of becoming my own healer. And the fact that reiki can be learnt in just a day (at least in the first level of training) doubled its appeal.

I was also beginning to mull over the idea that this might be something I could share with others. The words 'You don't have to just be a writer' had been spinning around my head since September. I was hoping this day of reiki training and attunement might become the start of something. This was just the first level of the learning process, but maybe I'd eventually become a practitioner and use reiki to help other people. I was stepping out of my comfort zone. It felt strange, but it also felt good.

There are different disciplines and branches of reiki and I'd chosen this one, traditional Usui reiki, for no reason other than that I'd had a good feeling about Jackie. And so far, that feeling was being proved right. I liked her instantly. She was softly spoken, calm and considered. Just being in the same room as her was slowing my mind down. She was also brilliantly down-to-earth. She'd sent me a message before I arrived, reminding me to bring some slippers to up the comfort factor, and she'd laid out a seriously impressive array of teas and snacks. She also didn't baulk when I eschewed the herbal tea options for the caffeinated version.

She was a good teacher, too. I realized I'd forgotten what it felt like to devote a whole day to learning something new, and not just because I had to write a feature on it the following morning.

I was learning reiki simply because I wanted to. And it was surprising how radical that felt.

When was the last time *you* devoted a whole day to learning something just for the joy of it? The more I sat in that room with Jackie, the more I thought that everyone should do this, all the time. And the more I thought that maybe everyone should learn reiki.

The training for this discipline of energy healing has three distinct levels. The first is Reiki Level One, in which you learn how to use reiki to treat yourself and your friends and family. Then there's

Level Two, which enables you to become a practitioner, register with official regulatory bodies and also offer distant healing treatments. The final stage is Level Three, which is the master level – reach this and you can also teach and 'attune' others looking to learn reiki for themselves.

Reiki Level One teaching sometimes takes place over more than one day but the content remains pretty much the same. Find yourself a teacher and you'll most likely learn about the principles and history of reiki, the auric field (the frequencies that make up your energetic aura), the chakra system of energy centres in the body and what it means to channel universal life-force energy.

When people talk about energy healing or offer treatments and therapies in this area, the words they use sometimes make it sound as though they are in possession of some sort of magical healing gift. However, the power of reiki doesn't actually come from the practitioners themselves. A reiki practitioner is simply a channel for the universal life-force energy that ramps up the body's own healing abilities. It sounded like something I could definitely get on board with. I mean, who doesn't want to be a channel for superpowers?

Jackie and I moved on to practising the hand positions typically used in self-treatments and treatments for others and talked about different approaches and uses for reiki. I loved the idea that you can use reiki to power up plants and pets as well as people, and that you can use it to charge crystals or add good vibes to a meal as you cook. It was all so easy, too. There are no symbols to learn in Reiki Level One (there are in the subsequent levels) so it's incredibly simple to get to grips with. In fact, it felt like the most natural thing in the world.

I still felt nervous about the idea of being 'attuned', though. What if it didn't work? What if I felt nothing? What if I laughed out loud in the middle of the process? What even was the process?

When the time came, Jackie asked me to sit on a chair in the middle of the room and take a few deep breaths with my eyes closed. She explained what she was going to do, which was essentially move around me making various hand movements and symbols to transfer the reiki to me. It took just a few minutes and I was amazed to find that I really could feel the difference. I felt calmer. I felt more peaceful. I felt as if something in me had shifted.

When Jackie asked me if I wanted to try a practice treatment on her in her little under-stairs treatment room, I forced myself to say yes, even though I was terrified it wouldn't work. Fortunately, my fears were unfounded. As soon as I got started, I knew I'd found a practice that I'd easily be able to incorporate into my everyday life.

As a recipient, I'd always thought that the biggest benefit of reiki was the long lie down and the power visuals I got when my mind relaxed, but this felt like so much more. I could actually feel the heat coming out of my hands. And I was sure I could feel the energy flowing through me as I moved my hands over Jackie. It felt pure and powerful and as if my mind was being opened up at the same time.

Knowing that I now had the tools to channel energy for myself and others felt like the kind of uplevel my life had been waiting for. I felt as if I'd been admitted into a secret society. Was this the ultimate in DIY magic?

When I got home and told my children what I'd been up to they both looked at me strangely and said they could do that already, as if it was obvious that anyone could. Then they started giving me mini treatments with their hands and, honestly, I could feel it. It made me wonder if it was even necessary to become attuned to a specific healing technique. It made me wonder if some people are born with the ability to channel energy in this way. It made me wonder if maybe we all are, if only we'd take the time to open up our energetic channels. Imagine! All that healing, calming power just waiting to be tapped into.

This felt like a world that I would, in time, go on to explore in much more detail but now wasn't really the moment. I lay on the sofa and let my youngest work her self-declared magic. There's nothing quite like the channelled energy of an over-enthusiastic seven-year-old to make you feel alive.

Do it yourself – learn reiki

If you're considering dipping a toe into the world of reiki, Reiki Level One is the place to start. Reiki's popularity means there are lots of teachers out there – which should make it easier for you to find the right one for you.

Learning reiki is a great way to make life feel a whole lot more magical and the benefits are numerous; the following are my top reasons to send yourself to reiki school.

◆ It's easy and accessible and Reiki Level One can often be learnt in a day

- The techniques will give you the tools you need to balance your own energy

- You'll learn about the chakra system

- Self-reiki helps with stress, relaxation and sleep

- You can use it on children, pets and stressed-out partners

- It'll make you feel like you have magic hands, and as if you've joined a secret society

SOLSTICE CELEBRATIONS & SEASONAL LIVING

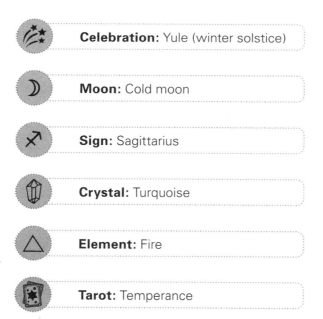

Celebration: Yule (winter solstice)

Moon: Cold moon

Sign: Sagittarius

Crystal: Turquoise

Element: Fire

Tarot: Temperance

Cool Yule

'Dwell on the beauty of life. Watch the stars
and see yourself running with them.'
MARCUS AURELIUS

We stepped outside into the inky evening darkness, wrapped up in scarves and gloves. The sky was clear enough for us to see the stars. My girls held the tips of their sparklers together as I shielded the flame of an almost spent plastic lighter I'd found in the back of the cutlery drawer. One flick. Another flick. A spark and a flame and a fizz of light. Squeals of delight and the smoky metallic aroma of cursive firework wishes scrawled across the night sky. Swirling names and smiling faces lit up by a golden glow.

It was 21 December, the winter solstice, the shortest day and the longest night, a press pause moment of deep darkness before the return to light begins. I'd long celebrated the summer solstice – it was my wedding anniversary, for starters – but taking time out to celebrate the winter version had always felt like a stretch too far.

December is the craziest month in a season of chaos, right? Decorating the house and panic-buying gifts and dropping all the balls you can think of and some you really hadn't. Who has the time to mark a pagan festival, long forgotten by most, with all that on their plate? Well, 12 months into my mystical year, it appeared that I did!

I lit another round of sparklers and surveyed the scene before me. I thought about posting a picture on Instagram but decided against it. That wasn't what this was about. When we headed back inside to light candle lanterns made from jam jars and masking tape, and clink glasses of mulled apple juice, I felt lit from within.

'I like Yule,' declared Cleo.

'Yule's cool!' said Lola.

'Isn't it just?' I replied.

A year earlier, this would never have happened. A year earlier I was falling apart and the idea of a teatime solstice celebration in my back garden would have definitely tipped me over the edge. That doesn't mean I didn't think about one, though. If I recall correctly, I was thinking about Yule quite a lot back then. A Yule *log*, to be specific.

A Yule log that sent me spinning into such a downward spiral of comparison and overthinking that a jigsaw puzzle could finish me off. Bear with me here – this will all make sense! And just in case we're at cross-purposes, I'm not referring to one of those chocolate-covered confections I used to will my parents to produce after Christmas dinner instead of the traditional pudding: I mean a full-on, drag-it-in-from-the-woods-and-set-it-alight-on-the-winter-solstice Yule log. Because somehow, amid the frazzled chaos of December 2017, I'd decided I really wanted one.

I was researching a magazine feature on festive traditions when I spotted the object of my desire. It was bedecked with holly, adorned with candles, anointed with fragrant seasonal oils and displayed in pride of place to mark the return-to-light magic of the winter solstice. There was an online 'how to' guide with step-by-step pictures and pages of notes.

This was no aspirational festive door wreath. This was no stylishly Scandinavian Christmas tree. This was no handmade children's advent calendar filled with sustainably sourced trinkets. Those things I could handle. I failed to pull them off every single year, but I could deal with it when I stumbled across them on other people's perfect Instagram feeds. But a Yule log? A Yule log was different.

Imagine being the kind of person who not only has it together on the whole December thing but also has time to carefully select a lump of wood to adorn for the winter. That has to be a person with their shit together, right? Someone who's blissfully in tune with nature and the seasons and the magic of life.

That person isn't running on empty just to keep up. That person – entirely fictitious and created in my own mind, to be fair – came to symbolize everything that was wrong with me and everything I wanted to change back in 2017. I wanted to be a Yule log person. But, well, I wasn't.

Things were really starting to unravel at the end of that difficult year. I was up to my eyes in Valentine-themed feature ideas for the magazine's February issue and hammering out online articles to see the website through Christmas. I had a huge amount of work to do before I could turn my attention to anything remotely festive. I was playing a game of take-it-to-the-wire roulette with my children's presents and only Amazon Prime could save me.

I'd purchased Christmas cards as though the investment alone was enough to get them magically written and sent to faraway friends and family. I was waking at 3 a.m. in a panic most days because I'd bought one of those artisan fill-it-yourself advent calendars on a whim but kept forgetting to put anything in the pockets. And I didn't have anything aesthetically pleasing or sustainable to put in them anyway – it was emergency Kit Kats from the snack cupboard all the way.

We didn't have any Christmas jumpers. We didn't have an Elf on a Shelf. Our door wreath was from Poundland and we had the kind of Christmas tree no one would show off about on social media. If I'd wanted to sum up my 2017 festive décor theme in one pithy sentence it would have been: 'I left the children in charge.'

My husband was working long hours at the hospital. I spent every spare moment typing frantically. And the school emails never stopped — raffle tickets, hampers, carol concerts, and cake stalls that needed to be manned at the winter fayre. If someone had suggested I throw a spontaneous festive soirée for a few friends, I would have had to fake my own death. Thankfully, no one did. They knew better than that. But I did get invited to one.

My friend Lucy is the queen of Christmas. And my word, she makes it look easy. If I was going to find my Christmas 2017 spirit anywhere, I reckoned it was round her house. So when she invited me over for some 'nearly the end of term' festive drinks, I ditched the laptop for the afternoon and dug out a sequinned cardigan.

'You looked stressed,' Lucy said as she opened her perfectly decorated front door.

'I am!' I replied. 'My Christmas spirit is at approximately zero.'

'I'll sort you out,' she said, handing me a glass of champagne.

She did, too. It's impossible not to feel festive when you're surrounded by chic Christmas jumpers and Michael Bublé on a loop. It was all so perfect. The beautifully decorated tree. The crackling fire. The carefully arranged platter of local cheeses. The cranberry-studded crackers in their fancy metal tin. The friends, the fun, the festive buzz.

Lucy was relaxed and radiant. Lucy had finished her Christmas shopping weeks earlier. Lucy had worked out that every child on the planet was going to want a Hatchimal that year at a point when it was still possible to buy one. Lucy was good at this stuff.

Lucy had already moved on to planning her New Year's Eve party. Lucy was offering to help out with the kids so I could get my work finished sooner. Lucy was lighting expensive scented candles. And opening another bottle. And refilling my glass. Again. I was feeling better by the minute. Until she got out the jigsaw – a 1,000 piece Christmas jigsaw.

'If anyone wants to help me get started on this, feel free!' she said. I raised an eyebrow.

'It's an annual tradition!' she laughed.

'But have you ever finished it?' I asked.

'Of course! Every time!'

A bloody Christmas jigsaw. It was the Yule log all over again.

Of course, I knew that everyone's life is different. I knew that we all have different responsibilities, different problems and different crosses to bear. I knew that just because something looks perfect, doesn't mean it is perfect. And I definitely knew that some people are just better organized than others. But right there and then, the idea that I might ever live in a world where I not only bought Christmas jigsaws as part of a quirky annual tradition but also got round to finishing them, sounded about as likely as moving to the moon.

And yet still, I wanted in. I wanted to be that vision of festive calm. I wanted the log! I wanted the jigsaw! I wanted it all! Or maybe I just wanted my life to be different. I knew I never again wanted to feel so stressed in the run-up to Christmas.

It wasn't just Christmas, either. I was looking forward to waving goodbye to everything about 2017. It was a year that had left me anxious, exhausted and sad. But it was also the year I found those tarot cards in the basement, so you know what happened next.

By the end of 2018, the positive effects of my year of mystical adventures had been revealing themselves to me for months; however, it wasn't until I starting comparing Decembers that I knew I could call it: my mystical year really had changed my life.

For all its twinkly lights and pleasingly mulled beverages, the season of goodwill can be a tough one. Perhaps it's tough for you? Perhaps your family doesn't fit the neat nuclear vision you see in the movies? Or perhaps you're being pulled in too many different directions? Maybe you're overworked or underpaid, and exhausted from trying to do it all?

Perhaps you're living through grief or depression or financial hardship? Maybe you don't even celebrate Christmas (not that anyone ever seems to notice)? It's easy for whatever you're going through to feel a hundred times worse when the people around you are high on eggnog. I get it. I've been there. I've driven myself to distraction over an internet Yule log. It certainly didn't occur to me that the solution to my seasonal stress wouldn't be so far removed from one.

When I really thought about it, what that comparison spiral Yule log symbolized wasn't a perfect human with all their festive ducks in a row – it was something more straightforward. Or, more accurately, it was exactly what it was: a symbol of the changing seasons and the turning of the Wheel of the Year. A symbol of the magic of nature doing its thing, as it does every year, whether we're too stressed to bear witness to it or not.

I'd reached the end of my mystical year and my life felt better on every level. I'd slowed down. I felt calm. I was happy.

I'd begun to notice the seasons again, and in that I found the easiest magic of all.

How often do you take the time to stop and notice the changing seasons? I know it can be easier said than done. Sometimes life races past so fast it's hard to find the time to breathe, let alone pay attention to the first falling leaves. I've spent many a winter workday logging on in the dark and off in the dark and barely registering the daylight in between.

As my mystical year entered its final weeks and I skipped into December calmer than ever, I found myself reflecting on this natural wonder that had been there all along. The wonder of nature, the changing seasons, the ebb and flow and cycles of life that witches and pagans and wise women and shamans had looked to for magic since magic began. Magic I'd let slip through my stressed-out fingers until my mystical toolkit pointed me in the direction of life in the slow lane.

Once it all came together it made total sense. I might not have tuned in to its power until now but this sort of seasonal magic had always been there. It was in the budding of spring and the hazy warmth of a balmy summer's evening. It was in the letting go of autumn leaves and the quiet solitude of a snow-capped winter hillside. It was there in the moon cycles I followed and the seeds I planted and the grass I walked upon barefoot.

It was there when I swam in the sea or sank my toes into sand or gazed up to watch the clouds float by. It was there when I woke up early to watch the sun rise and when I clinked a glass in its golden glow as it sunk below the horizon. And on that 21 December evening when I stepped into my back garden to celebrate the winter solstice, or Yule, with my girls, it felt stronger than ever. I promised myself I'd never again rush through a season, and that I'd celebrate all the festivals of the Wheel of the Year.

The northern hemisphere Wheel of the Year incorporates the ancient Celtic fire festivals of Imbolc (Brigid's Day), Beltane (May Day), Lughnasadh (or Lammas Day) and Samhain (Halloween) as well as four solar celebrations: the summer and winter solstices (Litha and Yule) and the spring and autumn equinoxes (Ostara and Mabon).

Today, these seasonal celebrations are marked by many modern pagans, druids, witches and practitioners of Wicca, as well as individuals seeking connection with the natural world. There are variations in the names, terminology and practices used by different groups but the principles behind the marking of these festivals remain broadly the same: a celebration of light and dark, ebb and flow, the elements, seasonal change and the magic of nature.

I already marked the summer solstice every year without fail – toasts raised to a Greek island wedding in the stretched-out light of the longest day. And Samhain, or Halloween, was an annual essential too, although the ancestor offerings (sweets, flowers, herbs, drinks) I once left out by my candles and tarot cards had given way to spooky plastic bats and fake blood make-up and the monster-shaped corn snacks my children adored. But that was it really. I'd never taken the time to celebrate the equinoxes, and Beltane, Imbolc and Lughnasadh had pretty much passed me by.

> *Perhaps we could all benefit from taking the time to celebrate the festivals of our ancestors.*

Celebrations of nature and life and magic that haven't been swallowed up by card companies and Amazon Prime and Black Friday special offers. I'm pretty sure that no one ever spent the spring equinox stressing out over canapés or falling into a social media comparison trap. There's something wonderfully easy and joyful in simply remembering what's gone before and what will forever continue to be; in knowing that it's winter but that it'll be spring again soon.

Of course, learning to slow down and live in alignment with the seasons doesn't have to mean celebrating the solstices or indeed any of the Wheel of the Year celebrations. There are many other simple ways to tune in to the world around you and allow yourself the space and time to notice the changing seasons.

For you, the magic of seasonal living might be in a bunch of nodding supermarket daffodils bought at the first sign of spring. Or in the cool thrill of an outdoor swim at the peak of summer. Perhaps you'll find it while collecting conkers as the leaves turn golden and the sun lies low in the sky. Or in the spindly tree skeletons left behind in a frosty winter park.

Or it might be even simpler than that. For you, living by the seasons might be a lifestyle choice that starts on the inside. It might mean eating seasonal food that leaves the lightest of footprints upon the Earth. It might mean planting seeds and watching them grow. It might mean choosing to make conscious decisions to shop small, buy organic and reduce, reuse and recycle.

It might mean giving yourself a break and trusting that a winter of rest and recuperation matters just as much as a spring full of blooming growth. Or seeing your own life as a series of seasons, each one as essential to the whole as the next. It might mean giving yourself permission to show up and fall down and get up and try again. Or allowing yourself to believe in something bigger – in the moon or the stars or the power of the universe.

I'd made it to the end of my mystical year and my life really did feel magical again. I'd done all the yoga and consulted the cosmos. I'd cast spells and manifested a swim in the Pacific Ocean. I'd communed with my spirit guide and created my own rituals. I'd got to grips with crystals and tuned back in to tarot. I'd learnt to trust my own intuition. And I could channel life-force energy through my hands like a superhero.

> ✧ *I wasn't sure which mystical moment had turned my life around, but the steady magic of slowing down was the thread that connected it all.*

I'd found many ways to go slow in my year of mystical adventures but the easiest way of all required nothing more than a glance at the sky, the trees, the world and its weather.

Does your life feel like winter right now? Do you need to retreat? Or maybe you're in the full bloom of summer, high on life and love and potential. Wonderful, woeful or somewhere in between – however you feel at this moment in time, you can guarantee that it won't last forever. Not exactly as it is right now. Bad days become good days. High spirits descend. Mad love becomes something solid. Hearts break and get put back together. Children grow up. And so do adults.

This isn't about creating something perfect and impervious so you never have to feel sadness ever again. And it isn't about ripping it all up and starting again (unless that's what you want to do). It's about putting a shine on what you already have and finding a way to make your spirits soar.

It's about finding your own way, in your own world and making your own life feel magical again. A life that feels like it truly belongs to you. A life where you give yourself the space and time to feel good and think big and shine brighter than ever. A life where you take the bad days and roll with them and end up understanding yourself better. A life where you don't sweat the small stuff. A life where no matter what the world throws at you, you know in your heart that you'll rise again, just like the sun does every morning.

More than ever, as another New Year dawned, that's what I intended to do.

Do it yourself – celebrate the seasons

Taking the time to slow down, celebrate and soak up the seasons is an easy fast track to magic. Check out these ideas for commemorating the eight annual festivals of the Wheel of the Year.

Samhain (Halloween)

31 October–1 November. Carve pumpkins, do a Year Ahead tarot or oracle card reading, leave offerings for your ancestors.

Yule (winter solstice)

20–23 December. Build a bonfire, light candles, make lanterns, burn sparklers, celebrate the slow return to light.

Imbolc (Brigid's Day)

1–2 February. Light candles, make plans, spring-clean your space, plant early-sowing seeds.

Ostara (spring equinox)

19–21 March. Buy plants, sow seeds, arrange flowers, paint eggs.

Beltane (May Day)

30 April–1 May. Make a flower crown, get outside, gaze at the stars, place posies on the doorsteps of friends and family.

Litha (summer solstice)

20–23 June. Watch the sun rise, spend time in nature, light a bonfire, eat a feast.

Lughnasadh (Lammas Day)

1 August. Water your garden, talk to your plants, bake bread, invite friends over for dinner.

Mabon (autumn equinox)

21–23 September. Collect conkers and leaves, walk in the woods, drink mulled cider, practise gratitude.

New Year's Eve 2018

Bethan
So, I take it you totally nailed 2018, Emma?

And your life is now a vision of peace and perfection?

Just checking...

Is it too early to stake a claim on 2019 being MY year?
20:22

Sarah
Yeah, time's up, Howarth!
20:23

Fiona

It's NYE... go for it!
20:25

Sarah
Have you booked yourself in for a sound bath yet, Bethan?
20:25

Katherine
Or decided you come from outer space?
20:27

Fiona
Where is the moon, Bethan, where is the moon? If there's one thing I've learnt it's that this is KEY!
20:31

Emma
LOL. It's waning. In Scorpio! And it's already next year here in Sri Lanka!
20:34✓✓

Bethan
OMG! Sunshine! So jealous! That whole manifesting thing really worked, didn't it?
20:35

Emma
It would appear so! Though the magic that is a very generous trip-booking mother-in-law may also have played a part!

Get on it, Bethan! And the rest of you!

I've already asked the universe to sort you all out, obviously!

20:36✓✓

Sarah
Awesome. I'll take a month in a spa!

20:39

Bethan
I'll come with you! But I'll also need a full-time nanny. Per child.

20:40

Fiona
And a butler?

20:40

Bethan
If you insist!

Don't think you can jump the New Year manifestation queue just because you're already in 2019, Emma!

20:42

Emma
Wouldn't dream of it. I've already got everything I need.

20:43✓✓

Sarah
So spiritual!

20:45

Fiona
A year of mystical thinking will do that to a girl!

20:45

Bethan
Or maybe she's just smug from Sri Lanka!

20:50

Emma
🙏☀️🙏
Definitely both. Now, who wants a picture of the dessert buffet?

20:51✓✓

Epilogue

MY MYSTICAL LIFE

Imagine my surprise when I reached the end of 2018 only to discover that I still wasn't perfect. I was, of course, outraged! My alarm was set for 6:30 every morning and yet meditating with the sunrise remained a strictly ad hoc affair. I was still very much at one with my iPhone's snooze button.

I was also a long way from mastering a crow pose during my yoga sessions. And I hadn't yet become the kind of mother who meets her children at the school gates bearing homemade organic snacks. I didn't live in a perfect house by the sea. My attempts to become vegan were constantly being sabotaged by halloumi. And my wardrobe remained a Lululemon-free zone. I may have been calmer, happier and convinced that the universe was on my side, but I was also still me. Who'd have thought it? And who'd have thought that two years later I still wouldn't have it all nailed?

As I write this epilogue at the tail end of 2020 – quite possibly the strangest year any of us has ever had – Best Life Me is still missing in action. The good news is, I'm more certain than ever that she wasn't who I was looking for. I set out to find inner peace and make life feel magical again, not to become a flawless human being. And I think we can all agree that Best Life Me sounded pretty intolerable.

When I wrote about modern life having us over a barrel at the start of this book, I was looking back on a time when I was in a very different place to the one I'm in now. I was sad, exhausted, burnt out and forever running to keep up. I felt like I was missing a trick. As if there was some secret formula I could unearth to reveal miracle solutions to everything that kept me awake at night.

Work, stress, worry, feeling that I wasn't good enough and that I didn't fit in, wondering if I needed to get out of bed and check the oven was off for the second time that night. I wanted to run away, but I couldn't. I wanted a break from it all, but I couldn't do that either. I wanted my life to be different, but I didn't know how to change it. I wanted to feel better. I wanted to be happier. I wanted to find my people. I wanted to find inner peace.

I also harboured a secret fantasy that if I did manage to find some elusive state of zen, I'd magically morph into someone who had her shit together. Well, just in case any doubt remains, that person doesn't exist. And if I learnt anything in my year of mystical thinking it's that perfection isn't just overrated, it's impossible.

For every seemingly flawless spiritual being posting about clean living and moon magic and *#goodvibesonly* on social media, there's a person behind the scenes thinking about ordering Domino's and bunking off their yoga class. And there's nothing wrong with that. The idea that seeking a spiritual path or embracing mystical practices might morph into another load of To Dos on a list is more than I can bear. It's also the reason I wanted to tell this story. Because while you might find guidance, tips and recommendations among the pages of this book, that's what I want it to be first and foremost: *a story.*

Finding my magic

At the start of this book I explained that I was no guru, and I stand by that to the end. This is simply a story about what happened to me and how I found a way to make my life feel magical again. A story about the journey not the destination. A story that says to hell with toxic positivity and Insta-perfect ideas about sunset yoga and elaborate rituals and living the dream on a desert island.

This is a story about taking on the practices that work and not worrying about the ones that don't. A story about messing up and getting it wrong and dropping a whole lot of balls. A story about finding magic without changing everything right now and all at the same time. A story in which there's no big, dramatic revelation or life-altering moment (other than a pack of cards in a dusty basement) – just small steps squeezed in between the mess and the magic of everyday life.

We're all evolving and changing and learning, and why would we want it any other way? Why did I ever think I wasn't good enough in the first place? In a year filled with yoga and meditation, rituals and magic, I found a way to slow down, banish the burn-out, look within and actually like what I found there. I evolved, I changed and I learnt. I tried, I failed and I tried again. I found my own kind of magic. And I had great fun doing it.

> *Best of all, I discovered that most of the answers I was looking for were right where I already was.*

I found my magic in the quiet routine of candlelit Monday-night yoga – forever marked in my diary in permanent ink. I found my magic in the inhale and exhale of regular meditation – just not at sunrise, okay? I found my magic in the vibrations of crystal bowls and in tarot card pulls and in laughing children covered in bathtime bubbles. I found it in lighting candles and stirring tea and writing missives to the moon. I found it by allowing myself to believe in it all over again. I found it in the great outdoors, in the sky, in the Earth and in the trees.

But most of all, I found it by paying attention, remembering who I was and tuning in to what really mattered to me. I found it by looking inwards for answers instead of outwards for approval. I found magic because I *looked* for it.

And that's what I hope this book will encourage you to do. I hope that if you feel the call, you'll set out on your own path to inner peace, and that you might find you enjoy exploring the mystical world as much as I do. I hope you'll feel empowered to do that regardless of your circumstances or current life situation. I hope you'll start where you are and do what you can. I hope you'll find a way to squeeze the magic in between work and life and responsibilities that don't stop just because it's a new moon. I hope you'll discover that the path to inner peace really doesn't have to involve dramatic revelations or distant shores or expensive guidance for which you don't have the budget.

I hope you'll manifest your heart's desire and believe in better things. I hope you'll feel your own power. I hope your life will feel magical again, too. And one day, I hope that you might also share your story and make someone else feel less alone.

As 2019 dawned, I knew it would be different. I could feel it. I'd never felt happier to just see where life took me. And to trust that it'd take me where I was meant to go. And that's exactly what happened…

I didn't know when I was making wishes on the moon in 2018 that I'd end up using my love of all things lunar to bring people together in real life the following year. I wrote my first new-moon meditation as 2019 dawned and by March I was gathering friends in my living room for my very first ritual. I squeezed yoga mats, cushions and blankets into every square inch of space, borrowed beanbag eye pillows from my yoga teacher and went to town on the candles, cacao and vegan banana bread. It was magical. And it was the start of something special. By the beginning of that summer, I was running regular new and full moon rituals for groups of soul seekers in the very same studio I'd hidden at the back of for yoga when my mystical year began.

I also didn't know back in 2018 that reigniting my love of astrology would land me a horoscope column for one of my favourite magazines, *Glamour UK*. When the universe works to deliver you the most enjoyable writing gig ever it makes it very easy to believe it's got your back.

As my mystical year came to an end, I didn't know that I'd go on to complete my reiki training to practitioner level or learn to teach meditation. And I didn't know that I'd one day run vision-board sessions for a local community project or go into my children's school to show classes of eight-year-olds how to meditate with crystals.

I didn't know that I was someone who could bring people together or stand at the front of a room and explain moon cycles or oracle cards in a way that others could easily understand. I didn't know that I was someone who could talk on the radio about finding the magic in life, or that I'd be brave enough to ever show my face on

Instagram. I'd never have known I could be anything other than a solitary writer sat behind a laptop for all eternity – which to be fair, I still also am – if I hadn't set out to discover (and rediscover) the mystical world.

Of course, embracing the mysteries of the mystical world doesn't have to end in moon rituals and writing horoscopes. That's just me filling in the blanks in case you're interested in what happened next. The most life-changing part of my mystical year was, of course, the difference it made in my personal life. Without my year of mystical thinking I'm not sure whether I'd have realized how much my two girls needed a mother who not only works hard and achieves things but also loves her own life. I don't think I'd have realized how much they needed me to show them the magic of a sunset or the beauty of a sprouting seed or the need to slow down when it all gets too much.

And without seeing me move into the slow lane, I'm not sure that my husband would have taken his own work–life balance to task, reducing his hours to spend more time with his mother, his children and me.

Without my mystical year, I know I wouldn't have made the friends I've made or genuinely found my people. And I definitely wouldn't have written this book.

A mystical call to arms

I'm not sure whether this final chapter ties everything up with the kind of neat bow that years of feature writing have taught me to seek in a conclusion. But I think that might be the point. I'm still evolving and I'm still changing and I'm still making mistakes. And having lived through the health scares, homeschooling and wake-up calls of the year that was 2020, I think we've all come a bit closer to understanding what really matters most. Especially those of us who have lost loved ones. I think perhaps we've all also felt the need for a little more magic in our lives. And a lot more inner peace.

Don't worry, this isn't about to turn into one of those inspirational missives about lockdown teaching us to stop and smell the roses. With two children off school and a doctor in the house, even mystical thinking couldn't generate quite that perfect a scenario for me, although we found our way all the same. And some of the positives that came out of those strange months might be just what a newly inspired mystical thinker needs to get to work.

Amid all the loss and the tragedy, the coronavirus pandemic also showed us new ways of doing things. Ways to translate real-world experiences into online ones that often worked better than we thought they would. Don't get me wrong here, I love an IRL ritual or yoga class as much as the next person – the reason I started running moon rituals was because I wanted to go to one and couldn't find anything locally – but plugging myself into a screen in lockdown made me realize that doesn't have to be the only way.

I can't predict the future (no matter how many tarot cards I pull), but if it involves yoga teachers and healers and meditation experts offering more online options that open up spiritual experiences to those who might otherwise feel excluded (by location, finances or toddler bedtimes), that can only be a good thing.

 The mystical practices I discovered or rediscovered remain at the heart of everything I do today. They help. They work. They keep me sane.

I haven't stopped stirring intentions into my tea or lighting candles or practising yoga. Or turning to meditation when times get tough, or reading cards when I'm looking for answers. I always know which phase the moon is in and which planets are currently retrograde. I spend as much time outside as I can. I take things slow. I notice the little things. I pay attention to the changing seasons. I celebrate the solstices. I remember to breathe. I trust the universe. And I try to make a difference wherever I can.

I never want that To Do list of modern life madness I wrote at the start of this book to run through my mind again. And I never want it to run through yours, either. I might even rip that page out and burn it on the next full moon. The only list I want to run through my mind now is one full of magic and joy and potential and possibility. Think of the following parting paragraphs as my mystical call to arms; a blueprint for better; the start of something magical. Because this is the only way I want to live now...

Watch the sunset. Gaze at the stars. Attune to the moon. Hug a tree. Grow something from seed. Read a great book. Drink tea. Light candles. Create a morning routine that works for you. Try yoga. Meditate. Learn to breathe. Do something you've never done before. Bask in the sun. Look for a sign. Cook. Create. Play. Paint. But don't do any of that if it feels like a chore.

Swim in the sea. Walk barefoot on the Earth. Cry. Laugh. Reach out. Connect. Write your story. Share what you have. Make something more beautiful than it was before you started. Love who you love. Stand up for what you believe in. Be an activist. Fight for a cause. Listen to what children have to say. Tread gently upon the Earth. Treat people with kindness. Indulge your senses. Make time. Slow down. Relax. Be yourself. Tune in.

Listen to your inner voice. Trust the universe. Find your people and love them forever.

And most importantly of all...

Lie down more.

SPIRITUAL
SOURCEBOOK

Here, you'll find listings of resources to accompany each chapter of the book. These are by no means exhaustive – they're just my personal recommendations for the books, shops, websites, podcasts and Instagram accounts I think are worth exploring or following if you fancy digging a bit deeper into one mystical subject or another. I haven't read every word of every book listed here or listened to every episode of every podcast, but I believe they all have something to offer.

I've also included a few practitioners that I can personally recommend, as well as the odd recommendation from my trusted mystical friends. However, as with everything in the mystical world (and life in general), it's important to do your own research and follow your own intuition on what's right for you. But definitely go forth and explore.

January: Vision Boards & Downward Dogs

Read all about it

A Life Worth Breathing: A Yoga Master's Handbook of Strength, Grace and Healing, Max Strom; Skyhorse Publishing.
Far more than just a guide to the benefits of yoga, this book teaches how to use breathing and meditation to reach a whole new level of awareness.

A Yogic Path: Oracle Deck & Guidebook, Sahara Rose Ketabi and Danielle Noel; Alpha Books.
A beautiful oracle deck inspired by the ancient wisdom of the Vedas.

Every Body Yoga: Let Go of Fear, Get On the Mat, Love Your Body, Jessamyn Stanley; Workman Publishing.
Great for beginners or anyone who feels that yoga isn't for them, this is a positive, accessible book from a very inspiring teacher.

Yoga: A Manual for Life, Naomi Annand; Bloomsbury Sport.
This coffee-table book is an inspiring, easy-to-follow guide to making yoga part of your life.

Yoga for Everyone: 50 Poses for Every Type of Body, Dianne Bondy; Alpha Books.
Another great book for beginners that proves yoga isn't just for super-bendy, skinny people.

Watch party

I Am Maris; available on Netflix.
An inspiring documentary charting the journey of a young girl called Maris who heals anxiety, depression and an eating disorder with the help of yoga.

Yoga supplies

Lululemon; lululemon.co.uk
I mean, I can't not include them, right?! I still haven't made it into Lululemon land, although my sister-in-law swears by the buttery-soft Align pants and I'm always jealous.

Moonchild Yoga Wear; moonchildyogawear.com
I love everything about this small, conscious yoga brand (and not just because of the name). This is where I bought my yoga mat.

Yoga matters; yogamatters.com
The classic go-to – for teachers, studios and individuals alike – for mats, props and blankets in an array of beautiful colours.

Online classes

Triyoga; triyoga.co.uk
Sessions from these beautiful London studios are now available to livestream, so anyone can take part.

The Underbelly; theunderbelly.com
Subscription-based yoga from Jessamyn Stanley. You can also find her (and some great free sessions) on YouTube.

Yoga with Adriene; youtube.com/yogawithadriene
She has eight million YouTube followers for a reason! Free themed online classes for everything from back pain to broken hearts.

Instagram follows

I don't massively go in for following yoga accounts but these are a few of my favourite exceptions to the rule.

Adriene Mishler; @adrienelouise
The queen of YouTube yoga, Insta-style.

Bastard Yogi; @bastard.yogi
For the laughs.

Dianne Bondy; @diannebondyyogaofficial
Real-world inspo for every type of yogi.

Helen Bishop; @helenbishopyoga
All-round fabulous human, and my yoga teacher. She started running live online sessions during the pandemic and when life's normal runs wonderful annual retreats in Italy and India.

The Human Method; @thehumanmethoduk
Somatic movement and yoga from Nahid de Belgeonne.

Jessamyn Stanley; @mynameisjessamyn
All the inspiration you need to Just. Do. It.

Ravi Dixit; @raviyoga_goa
Dreamy travel pics and yoga inspo from London/Goa-based Ravi Dixit.

Official bodies

British Wheel of Yoga; bwy.org.uk
International Yoga Federation; internationalyogafederation.net

February: Sound Baths & Spirit Guides

Read all about it

Animal Speak, Ted Andrews; Llewellyn Publications.
   This was the book we used to look up our animals at the spirit guide session I attended.

The Seven Types of Spirit Guide, Yamile Yemoonyah; Hay House.
   Open your mind to the magic of spirit guides with this exploration of different types of cosmic helper.

There's an app for that

Synctuition
   Relaxation, 3D sound and binaural beats on demand.

YouTube follows

Soothing Relaxation; youtube.com/soothingrelaxation
   I often find myself returning to this account for easy relaxation music.

Instagram follows

Aisha Carrington; @aishacarrington_
   The coolest sound healer on the internet.

Alice Rose; @alicerose.space
   Kent/Sussex-based practitioner Alice runs monthly sound baths and healing circles both on- and offline.

Jasmine Hemsley; @jasminehemsley
   My go-to account for recipes, eco fashion and self-care wisdom; it's made even better by regular lunchtime sound baths on Instagram Live.

Tamara Driessen; @tamaradriessen_
   The spirit guide session I attended was hosted by Tamara. She sometimes runs similar sessions, so keep your eyes peeled.

Studios

Crystal Sound Lounge; crystalsoundlounge.com
London sound studio offering crystal bowl and gong baths.

Remind Studio; remindstudio.com
My go-to for crystal sound (and meditation) sessions in London. There's also an amazing shop on site.

Sound supplies

Crystal Singing Bowls; crystal-singing-bowls.co.uk
UK stockist of the stunning, and stunningly expensive, Crystal Tones crystal alchemy bowls. Be warned: you'll want them all.

Sound Travels; soundtravels.co.uk
Drums, chimes and crystal bowls – consider this brilliantly down-to-earth online seller your one-stop shop for all things sound.

March: Everyday Magic

Read all about it

The Universe Has Your Back, Gabrielle Bernstein; Hay House.
A brilliant starting point for anyone interested in trusting the universe and believing in signs.

Rise Sister Rise, Rebecca Campbell; Hay House.
A manifesto for a new world. I love this beautifully inspiring read.

Spiritual shops

The Atlantis Bookshop; theatlantisbookshop.com; @the.atlantis.bookshop
London's oldest independent occult bookshop.

Boudica's Botanicals; boudicasbotanicals
Etsy shop offering herbal bundles wild foraged in Scotland.

G Baldwin and Co; baldwins.co.uk; @baldwinsuk
Established way back in 1844, this is London's to-go purveyor of herbs, remedies and natural products. If you're starting out making your own teas, aromatherapy blends or candles this is a great place to start.

Haeckels; haeckels.co.uk; @haeckels
There's something special about the incense, candles and bath products created by this Kent-based brand. A sea witch's dream.

House of Formlab; houseofformlab.com; @house_of_formlab
Beautifully curated, Amsterdam-based spiritual supply shop.

Mama Moon HQ; mamamooncandles.com; @mamamooncandles
As well as shopping online, you can now book an IRL appointment with Semra Haksever at her magical East London space. My absolute favourite scented spell candles.

Neal's Yard Remedies; nealsyardremedies.com; @nealsyardremedies
With high-street shops in towns and cities across the UK, this is a great place to start for natural remedies, herbs and aromatherapy products.

SLC London; sheslostcontrol.co.uk; @slc_london
Super high-vibe lifestyle store selling ethically sourced crystals, tarot decks, books and more. The online offering is just as good and they also offer a huge array of top-notch in-person and online readings and mystical gatherings. Basically, The Dream.

Star Child Glastonbury; starchild.co.uk; @star_child_glastonbury
A trip to Glastonbury isn't complete without a visit to this magical shop selling herbs, oils, candles and incense. Brilliant online service too.

Starstuff; starstuffshop.com; @we_are_starstuff
If you live anywhere near Bridport in Dorset you're in for a treat with this magical emporium of spiritual goods. Also great for online shopping.

Treadwell's Books; treadwells-london.com; @treadwellsbooks
Magical and occult bookshop in London's Bloomsbury.

Instagram faves & follows

Alexis Smart Flower Remedies; alexissmart.com; @alexissmartflowerremedies
The best flower remedies I've ever tried and the most inspiring Insta dispatches from Joshua Tree, California.

Magic Organic Apothecary; moa.co.uk; @magicorganicapothecary
Natural and organic skin care inspired by herbal folklore, and my forever fave source of sense-stirring bath products.

Moon Mist by Paolo Lai; paoloreflex.co.uk; @paoloreflex /
@officialmoonmist
> *This high-vibe, small-batch aura spray made on the full moon by reflexologist to the stars Paolo Lai can make anyone believe in magic. I'm never knowingly without a bottle.*

Star Ametrine; starametrine.com; @starametrine
> *Magical herbal products made in the Cotswolds countryside by botanical alchemist Roberta. Beautiful teas, flower essences and ritual oils.*

Trip Drinks; drink-trip.com; @trip.drinks
> *Beautifully packaged and great-tasting CBD drinks and oils.*

Wild Planet; wildplanetaromatherapy.co.uk; @wildplanetaromatherapy
> *Aromatherapy oils and aura sprays by an independent Kent-based brand.*

Tea time

Tea Pigs; teapigs.co.uk
> *I'm obsessed with their chamomile tea pyramids. Handily available in supermarkets, so you can chuck a pack in with your shopping.*

Yogi Tea; yogitea.com
> *If you like your tea with a side of positive affirmation, this is the one for you. Interesting blends with a message for the day on each bag.*

Pukka Tea; pukkaherbs.com
> *There's nothing I don't like about this widely available Bristol-based brand. In fact, I never go to bed without a cup of Pukka Night Time.*

April: It's Just a (Moon) Phase

Read all about it

Moonology, Yasmin Boland; Hay House.
> *This brilliantly inspiring and accessible guide to working with the moon cycle is my go-to.*

Moonology Diary, Yasmin Boland; Hay House.
> *Never miss a moon – new, full or otherwise – with this inspiring diary. Also an Instagram must-follow @moonologydotcom*

Luna, Tamara Driessen; Penguin Life.
> *A beautifully written guide to using the power of the moon to live your best life, from healer, tarot reader and author of* The Crystal Code.

Lunar Living, Kirsty Gallagher; Yellow Kite.
> *This inspiring guide to working with the magic of the moon is a* Sunday Times *bestseller.*

The Moon Book, Sarah Faith Gottesdiener; St Martin's Essentials.
> *A guide to conscious living and lunar magic.*

Instagram follows

Alexandra Roxo; @alexandraroxo
> *American writer and spiritual teacher Alexandra Roxo (who guided my April new moon ritual) continues to push boundaries, create, and encourage others to step into their power. Author of the powerful call to arms F*ck Like A Goddess and creator of membership platform Radical Awakenings.*

Girl & Her Moon; @girlandhermoon
> *Moon memes galore.*

May: Don't Hate, Meditate

There's an app for that

Hay House Unlimited; hayhouse.co.uk
> *An array of magical audiobooks, meditations and podcasts in one handy subscription. Inspiration galore.*

Calm; calm.com
> *On demand recordings for sleep, meditation and relaxation. And if you've ever fancied a bedtime story from Idris Elba, Kate Winslet or Harry Styles you're in the right place.*

Headspace; headspace.com
> *Straight-talking meditation and mindfulness for better sleep, reduced stress and clear thinking.*

YouTube follows

Pure Rasa; youtube.com/organicheart
> *I love the guided meditations on this channel (so much so that I had to wean myself off them!)*

Instagram follows

Davidji Meditation; @davidjimeditation
Meditation inspo from US author and master meditator Davidji.

London Meditation Centre; londonmeditationcentre.com;
@londonmeditationcentre
Vedic meditation centre offering in-person and online teaching.

June: Play Your Cards Right

Read all about it

The Book of Tarot, Alice Grist; Piatkus.
A brilliant guide to using your intuition to read tarot. Also a wonderfully down-to-earth Insta follow @alicegrist.

The Book of Tarot, Danielle Noel; Andrews McMeel Publishing.
A guide to tarot by the creator of The Starchild Tarot.

The Library of Esoterica: Tarot, Jessica Hundley, et al; Taschen.
A stunning illustrated coffee-table guide to the history of tarot.

Tarot & oracle decks

Modern Witch, Lisa Sterle; Liminal.
I love this super-cool, modern tarot deck.

The Starchild Tarot, Danielle Noel; Starseed Designs.
The most dreamily illustrated tarot deck I've ever seen and my current (possibly forever) go-to.

She Wolfe, Devany Amber Wolfe; www.serpentfire.ca
This stunning tarot deck can be difficult to source in the UK (it's occasionally in stock on Dutch site House of Formlab BV), but it's well worth hunting down if you can.

The Wild Unknown, Kim Krans; HarperElixir.
A striking modern tarot deck that works really well for intuitive readings.

Moonology Oracle Cards, Yasmin Boland; Hay House.
A brilliant way to attune more deeply to the moon – I love these oracle cards and use them all the time.

Work Your Light Oracle Cards, Rebecca Campbell; Hay House.
Still my go-to for big questions, small questions and starseed adventures in outer space.

Instagram follows & readings

Tamara Driessen; @tamaradriessen
Known for her intuitive tarot readings – now mostly available online.

Tree Carr; @treecarr
Author of lucid dreaming guide Dreams, *Tree Carr is always inspiring. She does regular reading sessions and workshops at SLC London and runs sessions online too.*

Victoria Maxwell; @newagehipster333
There's a real community feel to the Witch, Please *author's Insta account, with weekly card pulls and mystical inspo galore. She runs some brilliant online spiritual development circles too.*

Podcasts

Tarot for the Wild Soul, Lindsay Mack.
One of my favourite tarot podcasts, with episodes covering everything from numerology to eclipses.

July: Garden Shed Healers & Crystal Myths

Reiki

Read all about it

Judgement Detox, Gabrielle Bernstein; Hay House.
It isn't about reiki, but this thought-provoking guide to releasing the beliefs that hold you back is what I was reading in July.

Self Reiki, Jasmin Harsono; DK.
This easy-to-read guide is great for reiki beginners. Author and reiki and sound practitioner Jasmin Harsono is also well worth an Insta follow @emeraldandtiger.

Watch party

Heal; available on Netflix.
> An interesting and thought-provoking documentary about healing and the power of the mind.

Instagram follows & practitioners

Claudia Bonney; @claudia.bonney
> Artist and reiki master Claudia was the practitioner who gave me my very first reiki treatment. She now creates the most magical totemic paintings inspired by saints, myths and magic, as well as offering reiki mentoring.

Dot Winter; @dwinterspiritualhealer
> I discovered Dot in 2019, so while she doesn't feature in the book, she's very much been a part of my mystical journey since. I love her treatments (she's based in Kent) and her Insta is a never-ending source of inspo. She also offers training and distant healing sessions.

Myra Antonia; The Lyran's Den; @starseed_akasha
> Meditation guide, channel and reiki practitioner Myra Antonia offers relaxing recordings, downloads and plenty of magic on Instagram. She also offers treatments and training in and around Kent/East Sussex.

St Leonards Reiki; @st_leonards_reiki
> I loved learning reiki with the super grounded and down-to-earth Jackie Ward. Recently relocated to France, she offers reiki and EFT treatments as well as training and distant healing.

Official bodies

UK Reiki Federation; reikifed.co.uk
> A handy resource for anyone looking for a registered reiki practitioner for treatments or training.

Crystals

Read all about it

The Crystal Code, Tamara Driessen; Penguin.
> I bought this book the second it was available for pre-order in 2018 and love its beautifully inspiring imagery. An accessible, easy-to-use guide to getting to grips with crystals.

The Power of Crystal Healing, Emma Lucy Knowles; Pop Press.
> *The first book on crystals I read and an important part of my mystical year. This is a brilliant starting point for anyone who wants to know how to make crystals a part of their life. Author and healer Emma Lucy Knowles is an Instagram must-follow. Find her @your_emmalucy*

Instagram follows & readings

AndCrystals; andcrystals.com; @andcrystals
> *Crystal healer and sound practitioner Katie-Jane Wright sells crystals, runs courses and is the author of* Crystals: A Conscious Guide.

Odelia & The Crystals; odeliaandthecrystals.com; @odeliaandthecrystals
> *Odelia offers online crystal readings (like the one I described in the July chapter) and general Instagram inspo.*

Soulstice London; soulsticelondon.com; @soulsticelondon
> *A reliable source of crystal magic.*

White Witch Co; whitewitchco.com; @whitewitchco_
> *Traceable crystals and ritual kits by Olivia Wheldon. Also a brilliant Instagram account for crystal fans.*

See also Sourcebook recommendations for March, especially SLC London and Starstuff – two brilliant bricks-and-mortar shops that are great for buying crystals

August: Written in the Stars

Read all about it

I have too many books on astrology to list them all here, but these are my favourite recommendations for beginners.

The Birthday Book, Shelley Von Strunckel; DK.
> *A brilliantly fun book that charts personality traits and compatibility for every single birthday of the year.*

The Library of Esoterica: Astrology, Andrea Richards, et al, Taschen.
> *An inspiring coffee-table book on the history and magic of astrology.*

The Signs, Carolyne Faulkner; Penguin Life.
If there's a more perfect book for beginners wanting to learn more about their birth charts and themselves, I've not read it. The author is @carolynefaulknerofficial on Insta.

You Were Born For This, Chani Nicholas; Yellow Kite.
An empowering modern guide to understanding the stars.

There's an app for that

Chani
Super insightful astro app by Chani Nicholas.

Co-star
I can't help but love this app. Its computer-generated content can be comically random at times (it once told me to avoid clowns for the day!), but it's a really fun way to tune in to the power of the zodiac on a daily basis.

Websites for birth charts

The following all offer free chart generators.

Astro.com
Long-running astrology site with chart generators and information galore.

Astro-seek.com
An easy-to-use source of astro information and chart generators.

Cafeastrology.com
This useful site is packed with astro information and also offers free chart analysis when you generate a chart.

Dynamicastrology.com
A modern and accessible chart generator with the option to upgrade to a well-priced premium version for more information. By Carolyne Faulkner, astrologer and author of The Signs.

Shopping

The Astrology Shop; londonastrology.com
London shop selling everything an astro aficionado could wish for.

Instagram follows & astrologers

Alchemise; @alchemise_
The best astro energy reports ever.

Alice Bell; @stalkalice
Resident astrologer at British Vogue and one of my fave astro instagram follows. Also offers readings. Alice is brilliant at explaining astrology in a fun and accessible way, and her predictions are spookily spot on.

Chani Nicholas; @chaninicholas
Sign up to Chani's newsletter for weekly horoscopes.

Francesca Oddie; @francescaoddieastrology
Super knowledgeable astrologer offering readings, courses, events and a never-ending stream of info on Instagram. She also creates beautiful art print charts that make great gifts.

Glamour UK; @glamouruk
Check out my monthly horoscopes for Glamour UK online at glamour.co.uk

The Numinous; @the_numinous
Super cool astrology site that also publishes books for the 'Now Age'.

Shelley Von Strunckel; @vonstrunckel
I've read Shelley's horoscopes religiously for decades and she's been writing them for even longer. Her Instagram is a joyous mix of sunrises, sunsets and zodiac musings. You can order charts from her online.

September: Empaths, Intuition & Indecision

Read all about it

The Empath's Survival Guide, Judith Orloff; Sounds True Inc.
The source of the empath questionnaire I completed, and much more besides.

The Life-changing Power of Intuition, Emma Lucy Knowles; Pop Press.
An insightful guide to tuning in and transforming your life.

Life coaching

Action Woman; actionwoman.co.uk; @action___woman
Super intuitive and accessible coaching from Emma Jefferys.

Go Brand Yourself; gobrandyourself.uk; @gobrandyourself
Niki Jones is a coach and personal branding expert.

White & Lime; whiteandlime.com
Life coaching and people development consultancy from my September chapter Diet Coke and crisps-bearing friend Fiona Gilkes.

October: Magical Places

Should you ever find yourself in Australia's Byron Bay for the weekend...

Byron Medicine Wheel; byronmedicinewheel.com.au
A great spot for tarot readings, reiki and alternative therapies.

Sattva Yoga; sattvayogabyron.com.au
Based in Byron Bay Surf Club, right by the beach, this is a great place to practise yoga with a wave-crashing soundtrack.

November: DIY Magic & Spiritual Activism

Read all about it

Craft: How to be a Modern Witch, Gabriela Herstik; Ebury Press.
An easy-to-read, fun guide to modern witchery for anyone intrigued by the workings of the craft.

Everyday Magic, Semra Haksever; Hardie Grant.
The first of three books by Semra Haksever (also known as Mama Moon) and one of my favourites. Packed with spells and advice and down-to-earth magic tips.

HausMagick, Erica Feldmann; Ebury Press.
This brilliant book covers everything from clearing and crystals to communing with your pets. It's a witchcraft 101 for your home.

Initiated: Memoir of a Witch, Amanda Yates Garcia; Sphere.
An inspiring and beautifully written memoir of witchcraft by the Oracle of LA. The best book about being a witch I've ever read.

Witch, Please, Victoria Maxwell; HarperCollins.
A brilliant and inspiring guide to witchcraft, empowerment and living a mystical life.

Must-visit

Museum of Witchcraft & Magic; museumofwitchcraftandmagic.co.uk; @museum_of_witchcraft_and_magic
A magical museum and shop in Boscastle, Cornwall.

For reiki information and resources, see the July Sourcebook recommendations.

December: Solstice Celebrations & Seasonal Living

Read all about it

The Almanac, Lia Leendertz; Mitchell Beazley.
Published annually, this beautifully designed book is packed with everything you need to know about seasonal living and Wheel of the Year celebrations.

Shinrin-Yoku: The Art and Science of Forest Bathing, Dr Qing Li; Penguin Life.
When it's too cold and rainy to get out among the trees, this is the next best thing

Lunar Planner, Seven Stars; seven-stars.co
I order one of these planners every single year without fail. Designed by modern witch Katie Smith (@sevenstarsco) and packed with seasonal info on moon cycles, tarot, witchcraft and astrology.

ACKNOWLEDGEMENTS

Many people told me I should turn my Mystical Thinking project into a book, but it took getting a Capricorn on board to actually make it happen. Massive thanks to Emma Jefferys for introducing me to one: Oscar Janson-Smith, my brilliant sea goat agent.

I'm so happy my work found its perfect home at Hay House. A big thank you to Emily Arbis, Debra Wolter, Lucy Buckroyd, Michelle Pilley, Lizzi Marshall, Jo Burgess, Tom Cole, Diane Hill and everyone else who's helped play a part in getting this book out into the world.

And now for the hard bit – if I've missed you out please know I'll be haunted by it at 3 a.m. for at least a decade.

A lifetime of love, thanks and in-jokes to The Alts: Bethan, Claire, Kat, Katherine, Fiona, Sarah and Annie (my chosen ones – FF Forever). And more where that came from to my teenage coven dream girls: Louise, Joanne, Jane, Claire and Julia.

Thanks also to the school-gate survival squad – you know who you are, but extra thanks to Alice (who told me to do it!), Ella, Emma, Rachel, Simone, Lucy, Laura, Kate, Jane, Susan, Nicole, Luci, George, Niki and Sophie for believing in this book from the get-go. Same goes for the whole Broadwater crew (especially Toby's print shop).

Thank you also to everyone who's ever attended one of my moon events or helped make them happen: Agatha O'Neill (fellow Piscean and my creative partner in crime), Alice Rose, Laura Parker, Paolo Lai, Charlie Fowler, Roberta Perrin, Donna McCulloch, Julia Maitland-Shadwell, Helen Bishop, Melissa Bandtock, Laura Swann, Natalie Mcilveen and Jaime Cooke – kindred spirits the lot of you.

Thanks also to Lizzy Winding, Leesa Whisker, Isabel Dexter and Estelle Lee for always getting it. And to the fabulous Bianca London for commissioning me to write horoscopes for *Glamour UK* – aka my dream job!

Major love and thanks to my family, particularly my amazing Mum, Jennifer Thomson, and Dad, Simon Howarth, for allowing me the freedom to go my own way. And a massive high-five to the sibling crew: Rebecca, Sarah and Jake. Thank you Erini for breaking the in-law mould with me and Phaedra for all the summer *shavasana*. Not forgetting the wise ones: Mary and Pat.

Most importantly of all, thank you to Lola and Cleo, the two most magical creatures I know. And, finally, Alexis – thank you for doing All The Things so that I could write this. You make me believe in better. Forever looks good on us.

And to you, fellow mystical thinker – thank you for reading.

Bring on the magic.

ABOUT THE AUTHOR

Agatha O'Neill

Emma Howarth is a lifestyle and travel writer, and *Glamour UK*'s monthly horoscope columnist. She was an in-house editor at *Time Out*, where she wrote and edited travel guides to Tokyo and Paris, and titles including *The Little Black Book of London*, *Parties*, and *London for Londoners*. She was contributing and digital editor at *Smallish* magazine and her work has appeared in publications including *The Telegraph*, *Metro*, *Project Calm*, *Metropolitan* and *Reclaim*. She's also a tarot card reader and reiki practitioner who runs down-to-earth guided moon meditation events.

 @mysticalthinking

 @mysticalthinking

 @MakeLifeMagical

www.mysticalthinking.com

HAY HOUSE
Look within

Join the conversation about latest products,
events, exclusive offers and more.

f   Hay House

   @HayHouseUK

   @hayhouseuk

We'd love to hear from you!